Extraordinary Comfort

Extraordinary Comfort

*The True Story of a Mother's Near-Death Experience
Meeting Her Stillborn Son . . .
And the People Healed by Her Story*

by

DAVID C. ASAY

WITH CHRIS HEIMERDINGER

Extraordinary Comfort: The True Story of a Mother's Near-death Experience Meeting Her Stillborn Son . . . and the People Healed by Her Story

Published by NewLight Publishing

Cover design copyright © 2014 by Rachael Gibson
Cover image: Aaron and Chelsea Reimschiissel's "Baby Born to Heaven," photographed by Heidi Vawdrey (used by permission)

ISBN: 978-1-63315-649-4

Printed in the United States of America
Year of first printing: 2014

To my mother,
Mary Lou Gurr Asay

and my brother,
Shawn.

I look forward to meeting you.

CONTENTS

ACKNOWLEDGEMENTS

I would like to express my sincere gratitude to the many people who contributed to the realization and completion of this book and to all those who kindly answered my phone calls and responded to my emails, willingly providing me with opinion, direction, and constructive critique.

I am most grateful for all of my brothers and sisters who witnessed our mother's sacred experience with me and especially to Randy, Connie, Becky, and Larry who contributed their eyewitness accounts and notes for use in this book. I love you all very much.

I would like to thank Ted Stoddard, who I affectionately refer to as my writing coach, mentor, and crony. I appreciate both him and his wife, Mary, as dear friends, and for their tremendous help and support of this project.

I am so very thankful for my five wonderful children, and especially for the twelve (including one more on the way) precious grandchildren they have given to me and Pam. They make getting old worth it. Special thanks to my daughter, Nicole, and her husband, Mark, for their unwavering support and belief in me and this project.

I feel extremely blessed to have met Melissa Ohden, who survived an abortion attempt and is now sharing a strong pro-life message to the world. I asked her if she would read the manuscript and give me her thoughts from the perspective of someone who survived an abortion. After reading it, she informed me that she too had lost a precious, unborn child to miscarriage.

I then asked if she might consider writing an afterword for this book, which she kindly agreed to do.

Thank you Melissa.

I would also like to thank Hana Haitenan and Stephanie Clarke for their writing and editing expertise and helping me get this project off the ground in the early days.

I treasure my friendship with Chris Heimerdinger and appreciate so much his guidance and great word-smithing talents to help me bring out the important message of this book in the best possible manner.

There are many others who deserve recognition for their kindness in helping me along the way with this project. You know who you are, and I thank you very much.

Finally and most importantly, this book would not be possible without the constant support (at least tolerance) of my wife Pam, my sweetheart, eternal companion, and "Wunkin." I love and appreciate her without bounds for her patience, wonderful insight, and constant faith in me. All my love forever.

David C. Asay

PREFACE

I'm a champion procrastinator. It's not a trait that I'm proud of, and I don't believe confessing it earns me any brownie points here or in heaven.

The truth is, I made a promise more than a dozen years ago with my mother to write this book. I made the same promise to my wife and other family members. My mother has since passed away. I thank God that I completed it while so many of the others are still with me in this life.

From the outset, I've been keenly aware of the ramifications that this story might have upon real people. I felt it could be a sincere source of knowledge and intelligence (because these two aren't really the same thing). Most of all, I wanted it to be a source of great comfort. I've known all along that it could change thousands, hundreds of thousands—perhaps even *millions*—of lives. I've also faced the reality that because of my procrastination, many lives that *could* have received this comfort, will not. This is something I just have to live with.

Thankfully, I believe in a forgiving God. He knew all my weaknesses and distractions even before I made my promises. So despite the guilt I feel for not acting sooner, I also trust His love and grace.

The *ramifications* of these events have always intimidated me more than the events themselves. I'm not a banner-waving, fist-pounding, "activist"-type person. Yes, I've always held strong opinions about family and religion, but I never wanted to "mix it up" with those who held different beliefs. I suppose with this book I may have to change some of that, but I won't like it. No matter how you cut it, this is an extraordinary story. A *true* story. My objective was to recount real events exactly as they happened, exactly as reported to me by eyewitnesses, and exactly as I witnessed them myself. For now, I hope readers will forget about the controversial stuff and just focus on the events themselves.

This book is about a miracle. Actually, *several* miracles. Most would refer to the central miracle—the one described by my mother—as a "near-death experience." We commonly use that term to describe dying—or *almost* dying—and being "brought back" to continue life on earth. I prefer the term "a visit to heaven." Honestly, I don't know if this realm *is* heaven or if it's just a way station of that ultimate destination. In either case, the term will suffice.

Some might say, "Ah, there's a gazillion near-death experience books. What makes *this* one different?" The answer is in the *emphasis*—just as it was with my mother. Also, I've included a very personal and difficult trial my own family endured to round-out the most significant themes. I know that many embrace near-death accounts as a reassurance that heaven exists. I suppose this might provide the same sense of security. But if that were my *only* goal, I don't think I'd have felt driven to complete this project. You see, I already believe in heaven. I don't need a near-death experience to reassure me. I wanted to offer a sense of comfort far more penetrating and universal, based upon the eternal nature of the family unit itself.

Admittedly, the story provokes many questions. I'm no less anxious than anyone else to receive the answers. More than anyone, these events belong to my mother. They were God's gift to *her*. She was the recipient and primary benefactor. But she also desperately wanted her story told—she just wasn't physically capable of doing it. That's why I naïvely promised to do it for her.

So this is for you, Mom. Sorry it took so long. It's my very first book, and might also be my last.

Now that it's done, I tearfully confess that she has been with me through much of the process. Without her nudging and prodding, even from the "other side," I'd probably still be procrastinating.

I hope the story I tell will inspire, comfort, and give hope to many lives, just as she envisioned. I suspect the message will be of particular comfort to mothers—women who have suffered indescribable, heart-wrenching loss—and then, in silence, asked the questions: "Will I ever . . . ? Can I ever . . . ? Would God allow . . . ? Does He understand . . . ?"

After reading *Extraordinary Comfort*, I sincerely believe the answer becomes a glorious and resounding YES!

David C. Asay
Nov. 2013
daveasay@gmail.com

CHAPTER ONE

The Phone Call

Saturday, April 4, 1998

Life's not always fair.
Sometimes you can get a splinter
even sliding down a rainbow.
—Terri Guillemets

*A*irports.

I believe airports are among the loneliest places on earth. The Hartsfield-Jackson International Airport in Atlanta must rank among the loneliest of all with its maze of isolated shuttles and terminals. Except in airports, I've never quite experienced the phenomenon of so many people in one place with so little interest in intermingling or acknowledging each other's existence. They remain like private islands, their force fields raised, impenetrable. Only a New York sidewalk or subway might compare.

In 1998, airports may have been lonelier than even today. Today 24-hour news constantly drones from televisions affixed to ceilings. Fingers flutter across the keyboards of electronic devices. There's even an occasional grin or laugh from someone viewing a YouTube clip. Still, an individual's force field and private space is no less impenetrable.

I've traveled a lot in my career. I used to own an RCA portable VHS player that ran on battery power. Now and then as I waited in airports, sometimes delayed for hours, I popped in a collage of comedy clips or a Star Trek movie featuring the original cast, and strangers would request to join me. A crowd would gather behind me. It pleased me to bring a little variety to the mundane experience of plane travel. However, on this warm spring day in April 1998, I'd brought no such devices. It was just me . . . and my thoughts.

The airport crowd seemed heavier than usual as I strode to my gate. I couldn't help but study the expressions of my fellow travelers, wondering if any of them were experiencing sorrow like I was experiencing. A middle-aged woman looked as if she had been crying for hours. Her tears had dried up, but the redness and puffiness remained. Perhaps her distress was worse than mine. I never bothered to find out. Like everyone else, I was in a hurry. Such a hurry.

"Flight 401 for Salt Lake City now boarding at Gate 18."

I moved to the end of the line of passengers. Boarding had ground to a halt as two elderly people in wheelchairs were being helped. For once, I felt no thread of impatience or irritation. I'd had some personal experience with wheelchairs. Well, not me—my mother. I pondered Mom's need for a wheelchair and felt grateful that I was able to walk onto the plane. Staring out the massive airport window, I noticed the angry gray swath of an oncoming storm. Astonishing how such an enjoyable, almost idyllic day had changed so dramatically.

* * *

"Nice shot, Dad!" Rob called out.

My son, Robert, and I couldn't have chosen a better spring morning to loosen up our swings on the driving range at the Champions Club, an upscale, semiprivate golf course in suburban Atlanta. It was an activity we'd engaged in much too infrequently during the previous stress-filled years. I watched my son hit a few balls, reflecting on how much he'd matured since being away from home.

His gawky teenage body had transformed into a rather handsome young man—well, as much as a father can judge such things. He was as tall as me—six-foot two, and—like the song says—"eyes of blue." He still had that mischievous smile—the same one he'd sported all his life and that I now considered one of his most endearing features.

"How's married life treating you?" I asked, grateful beyond words that he'd found such a lovely, wonderful wife who'd brought Christian faith, love, and stability into his world. Moreover, she'd given my trial-ridden child a reason to live.

"It's great, Dad. You know, I still can't believe how things have turned around for me."

I smiled, a mixture of many emotions. He interpreted only the most obvious one.

"I mean, really. Can you believe it? I have a beautiful wife who actually loves me. She *loves* me. Who'd have guessed that I'd ever . . . ?"

He broke off. His expression betrayed no emotion. Robert rarely allowed himself to go that far. He generally stopped long before revealing anything below the surface. He concentrated on placing his ball on the tee.

"Yeah," I said. "We're both pretty lucky that way." Now *I* was the one near emotion. I tamped it down.

Let me confess up front—I'm a lachrymose kind of guy. Tears come easily to me. Maybe that was because of events over the last decade. It doesn't matter. In any case, the "chip" inside me that once controlled my emotions broke along the way. I know some feel a man whose emotions aren't held tightly to the vest isn't a real man. I can't speak for those who hold such an opinion, and I admit, sometimes I've had mixed feelings about this tendency. Nobody wants to "lose it" in front of others. Yet, tears were such a healing part of my life. I was unashamed of the trait and wouldn't have traded it. At its core, these emotions were born out of love: Love for God. For my family. My mother and father. My wife and all five of my children. And right now, love for my son, Robert.

I thought again of how far we'd come. How far we'd *all* come. And in some ways, how far we might still have to go.

It was natural that my next thoughts were of Pam, my beautiful wife. In 1998, we'd been married twenty-eight years. She was indeed the love of my life, a diamond among gems, a true help-meet who'd remained at my side during some of the very worst trials I believe a family can endure.

"How about your job at Pep Boys?" I asked, wanting to restore casual banter. "Still going well?"

"Yeah. Surprisingly enough, I really enjoy it, Dad, though some days seem awfully long."

"You always liked tinkering with cars," I said, "for as long as I can remember."

When he was younger, he owned an old Datsun B210 and an *ancient* Volkswagen Beetle. He got a kick out of replacing parts or fixing frequent problems.

"Exactly," he replied, lining up the drive.

He swung and connected flawlessly. Golf had always been a bit of an obsession for me. For Robert, it was a fairly new game. Still, I could tell that he was a "chip off the old block"—pun fully intended. I determined to make this a monthly or bi-monthly bonding ritual with Robert, now twenty-four. To think there was a time, a very dark time, when I seriously questioned, and when *Robert* seriously questioned, if he'd ever live to reach the age of twenty-one.

I added, "I'm sure people appreciate an honest mechanic. Too bad you'll never fix that monster hook the same way you can expertly fix a wheel alignment."

Robert countered, "How are your plans coming along for straightening out your boomerang slice?"

We laughed. The laughter warmed me like the April sunshine. If anyone had told me years earlier that Robert and I would one day enjoy a game of golf on a nearly perfect Saturday morning, I'm sure I'd have responded, sadly, that such a scenario was quite unlikely. All that seemed far behind us. We'd made it! With God's tender mercies, my son had indeed grown into a caring and responsible young man.

Just as I pondered the joy and relief, my cell phone rang. I was startled at the disturbance. Nothing breaks the concentration of a perfect swing or a smooth putt like an insufferably loud cell phone.

"Why did I bring that along?" I complained to myself.

Another club member shot me a deserved, angry glare. Sheepishly, I apologized, "I forgot to leave it in the car." I reached into the cart for the phone and fumbled to find the button that would silence it.

As I studied the small screen, I noticed that it was my wife calling. I pressed "receive."

"Hi Pam. What's up?" I said a bit tersely, turning away from nearby golfers, hoping I wouldn't disturb them any more than I already had.

"David," she said with just enough emotion to evaporate any annoyance. "David," she repeated.

"What is it? What's wrong?"

She still struggled with her words. By now, Robert could see that something wasn't right. He moved to my side.

"It's your mom," Pam explained. "Your dad just called to let us know she's back in the hospital. It's serious. Dad said that if you want . . . want to ever see her again . . . you need to come as quickly as possible. It's not good. You need to get on a plane . . . soon."

"I'll be right home."

I hung up, then stared blankly at the screen. For an instant, my legs became like licorice ropes. Rob was right there to guide me down onto the seat of the golf cart.

"It's your grandma," I explained, tears pricking my eyes.

Robert nodded. He fully understood.

My mother, Mary Lou Asay, had been in and out of the hospital many times in recent years with a wide variety of ailments, including cancer that had necessitated a double mastectomy and various complications associated with diabetes. Something deep inside—something I couldn't explain—told me this visit to the hospital in faraway Provo, Utah, would be different. However, as it turned out, *not* for the reasons I'd expected.

My son, so unemotional when it came to his own inner pain, encased me in a hug as heartfelt as I'd ever known. Without words, he offered comfort and compassion. It was a moment that could be shared only between a father and his adult son. I'd have relished that moment longer, but I had to get home—fast. Plane tickets. Packing. Phone calls. Arrangements. All in record speed.

As I stepped through the garage doorway into my home, Pam greeted me with her ever-understanding embrace.

"What can I do?" she asked.

She was the practical one in our relationship. Even if I hadn't answered, she'd have gone right to work, doing what needed to be done. I secured a nonstop flight to Salt Lake City. We assembled a carry-on bag with a simple change of clothes and a shaving kit so I could zoom past baggage claim and hop into a rental car.

"Are you sure you don't want me there with you?" Pam asked for the third time.

"Honestly, I'd love to have you with me," I admitted. "But there's no telling how long . . . and the kids need you here."

"Just call and I'll be on the next plane. You know that."

"I do know it, sweetheart."

As we drove to the airport, my thoughts started racing. Yes, I was one of those cornball American men who truly loved his mother, who couldn't imagine life without the security of her wisdom, solace, and unconditional love— just in a phone call. Now I had to wonder what I would find when I arrived.

"Is this really 'it'? Will I have a chance to say good-bye? She's only sixty-eight." I was rambling, more to myself than Pam. "It doesn't seem real."

"I know, David. I keep thinking the same thing: it's not fair. But your mom's a fighter. She'll hang on. You'll make it there in time. I know it."

CHAPTER TWO

The Journey

*Here is the test to find whether
your mission on earth is finished.
If you're alive, it isn't.*
—Richard Bach

Safely on board the airplane bound for Salt Lake City, Utah, I placed the earphones over my head and played one of my favorite Yanni CDs. Within moments, I had faded into a world of images and memories.

"Oh, David, my pine son with pine peets and grass on his head."

I clearly heard my mother's voice. I might have even looked around to see if she was in a nearby seat, her voice was so clear and penetrating.

"My pine son with pine peets and grass on his head."

Mom had a distinctive voice—one whose resonance had never faded. She teasingly used to call me her "pine son with pine peets"—or rather, her fine son with fine feet. I wouldn't have admitted it when I was a boy, but her lighthearted words and tone and just the way light seemed to dance in her eyes were some of my most endearing memories. When no one else could make me laugh, Mom always succeeded.

I was raised in a large American family—three brothers and five sisters. In a family of that size, one might think that a random child could get lost in the hustle and bustle. Not so. My mother had her way of making every child feel unique and special, that each one of us had unique and extraordinary gifts that would make a positive stamp on the world. In my case, no one else had "pine peets and grass on their heads."

I marvel today how she juggled the duties and complexities of such a family. We lived in a house with three bedrooms and one bathroom. Let me repeat that—three brothers, five sisters, me, two parents, and *one bathroom*.

Childhood home - 3 bedrooms, 1 bathroom, 9 kids

At the time I thought nothing of it. This was my life, and it was nothing unusual. Our parents fought hard to make life better for their children, and then we fought hard to make life better for ours. Somewhere along the way, this effort to make life better for our kids transformed into video games, computers, big screen TVs and personal electronic devices. These things were so cool, and our children's faces lit up when they saw them. We wanted to make our children happy. At what point did making our children happy also entrench them in a state of entitlement? At what point did we "over" love them and begin to hurt them, allowing them to become isolated physically and emotionally—not only from society, but from *us*, their parents? I'll leave that conundrum for others, those with a lot more letters after their names. For some reason—even though I was one of nine children—no modern gadgets or attitudes had diminished my devotion to Mom.

I know how over-sentimental that sounds to some. I've met people whose feelings for their mothers—the people who brought them into this world—aren't positive at all. Who'd have imagined a time would ever arrive when a child's devotion and responsibility toward his parents was "out of style"?

Of course I knew it wasn't really Mom's voice I'd heard—just a deep desire to be with her, holding her hand. I wanted to hear her singing her silly songs that made me laugh until my stomach hurt. I wanted to be a teenager again, coming in late from a date and finding her waiting for me in the dimly lit living room with her loving smile and sparkling green eyes, ready to hear every tidbit of my exciting evening.

Most kids might feel reluctant to confide such things to their mother. With my mom, it felt completely natural. I guess that in many ways, Mom never really grew "old." Not mentally, not in the way other mothers sometimes grew stuffy and disinterested. Mom immersed herself in all of the innocence and intrigue of teenage romance and was always full of advice on how to keep the experience "fun" and not get carried away with the ego-driven games that often caused so much pain for my teenage friends.

Once, I dated a girl who lived in our neighborhood. Mom thought she was wonderful. But on a date, as soon as we were alone, she became very aggressive—a bit too much, based on the standards my parents had taught me. We broke up and Mom was so disappointed. A short time later, this same girl became pregnant. I told Mom, "*That's* why I broke up with her." She was shocked, but happy that I'd shown such wisdom.

On a different date with a girl from a nearby town, I was invited to go out to eat with her family at a formal restaurant. For my family, an outing to Arctic Circle was a rare treat, so I already felt completely out of my element. They insisted that I order anything off the menu. After carefully studying the menu, I said, "I think I'll have the filet mignon. I haven't had fish in a long time."

Everyone, including my date, laughed so hard they were falling off their chairs. Finally, my date told me filet mignon was steak, not fish. I shrank down in my chair the rest of the evening. Filet meant something besides fish? After relating the story later to my mom, she comforted me in my awkwardness. She laughed and got me laughing as well.

There was no one else in my life who would sit with me and talk about whatever was on my adolescent mind into the wee hours of the morning—conversations I'll treasure forever.

Memories like these, along with the soothing music on my CD player, soon left warm tears moistening my cheeks. The flight attendant with the snack cart respectfully passed by without disturbing me. Scenes flashed across my mind like photos in one of those old View-Master toys. I thought about Mom in the kitchen on Saturday mornings, her apron covered in flour, as she pounded and kneaded enough dough to make exactly enough bread to last the entire week. The aroma of baking bread wafted through every room of the house. Ah, the pleasure of biting into bread so hot and fresh, it burned the tips of my fingers.

"Remember, this *has* to last us all week," Mom would scold. Looking back now, I'm certain she baked enough for the week with an extra portion for a Saturday treat of "fry cakes" for her children. Even sitting on an airplane at thirty thousand feet my mouth started watering at such memories.

The four-hour flight passed more quickly than I could have imagined. I have a theory about time. When we're younger, our perception is expanded. As we grow older, that perception compresses. The clock or calendar may proclaim that four hours or four years have gone by, even if it feels like a quarter of that time. That's how it felt when the wheels touched down on the runway at the Salt Lake International Airport.

With long strides, I made my way through the terminal to pick up my rental car. It was a little before 8 p.m. in this time zone. I could make the hospital in an hour if I could just get my rental car. Here's where my theory about time falls apart. When it comes to waiting in line, it doesn't seem to matter if you're old or young—time expands. The wait for a rental car seemed like an eternity, though it was probably only fifteen minutes. I soon found myself on

Interstate 15 on the final leg of my journey. I had no way to call relatives or receive updates on Mom's condition. I could only pray she was still part of this world.

What a grueling day! When I'd awakened I had no particular plans except a relaxing golf game with my son. Twelve hours later, I was in Utah, driving south toward the hospital where my mother was in critical condition. I was on my way to face the unknown.

CHAPTER THREE

The Arrival

The walls of hospitals
have heard more prayers
than the walls of churches!
—Manasa Rao

*I*t was 9:00 p.m. when I stopped at the lobby desk of the hospital in Provo, Utah. My twelve hour odyssey from receipt of my wife's call until I'd reached my destination was at an end. Well, almost. I hadn't yet arrived at the room where Mom was assigned.

The entire journey I'd been concerned that the front-desk employee—no matter who that person might be—might be the individual who informed me that my mother had passed away. Not a family member. Not a doctor. But a hospital volunteer. This simply wouldn't have seemed appropriate. I wasn't sure about protocol—maybe they weren't *allowed* to say it.

The desk volunteer was young, clean, pretty, and full of polite formality. I hardened my emotions and asked her the room number for Mary Lou Asay. She typed the data into the computer, rechecked the spelling of my mother's name, and then waited for the information to appear on her screen.

It might seem funny, but I was holding my breath in trepidation. What would have been the politically correct way for a front desk volunteer to tell someone the person they'd come to visit was dead? Maybe it would be in the form of a euphemism—"I'm sorry. It says this patient has been moved to another part of the hospital." Or spiritual in nature—"I'm sorry, Mr. Asay. It says here that her body is still with us, but her spirit has ascended to a higher sphere." Perhaps they'd done it so often they'd grown callous—"Hmmm. Looks like you *juuust* missed her. If you hurry you might still get there before they wheel her body off to the morgue."

None of that happened. I was convinced she genuinely didn't know my mom's condition as she kindly provided directions to the correct floor. I thanked her and moved toward the elevators.

No matter how I tried to hide it, it must have been obvious how worried and tired I felt as the elevator door opened and closed on each individual level. My heart thudded as I reached the correct floor. I followed the numbers posted above each room and made inquiries at the nurses' station. Then I looked over my shoulder.

There was my family inside the nearest patient room. I recognized my father even with his back to me. He stood in the midst of several of my siblings: my older sister, Becky, my younger sisters, Connie and Celiene, my brother Chris, and their spouses. These siblings all lived in Utah. I was the first out-of-state family member to arrive.

Seeing my siblings caused a rush of warmth to course through me. I wasn't too late. Everyone hovered over a hospital bed. As I joined my family inside the room, the sight of Mom was disturbing. Her eyes were closed. There were tubes and IVs everywhere. She looked emaciated, weak, frail, just clinging to life. Over the past several years she'd been admitted many times, but never in such a serious condition where her life was hanging in the balance.

The first thing I heard was violin music. A dear neighbor of my parents, Cherilee, was softly playing some of Mom's favorite hymns. It takes considerable skill to play a violin in a tiny hospital room softly enough not to disturb the entire floor. Cherilee had this kind of skill. The first person I greeted was my father. He looked exhausted, red-eyed, and nerves frayed. We embraced, and he took my hand in both of his.

"Thank you, David," he said. "Thank you for coming."

I embraced and greeted each of my siblings and their spouses. Afterwards, my focus riveted on my mother. The tubes and IVs jarred me. This wasn't the last image I wanted to have of her. Surely this was not the woman with the fortitude to raise nine children in a three-bedroom, one-bathroom home—who could juggle schedules, feed, clothe, bathe, and love every child as if it was her only one. Mom had always had boundless energy and enthusiasm for life. Now all that appeared to be slipping away.

At that moment, I received a tender mercy. That's what I call God's little miracles. Mom opened her eyes. She became conscious. Despite her weakness and inability to speak, I could tell she recognized me. She looked deeply relieved that I had come. I held her hand tightly, trying to transfer the energy from my body into hers. And it seemed to work a little because her eyes looked bright as I leaned close to her and said reassuringly, "I'm here, Mom. And I love you."

She squeezed my hand to let me know she understood. I continued trying to "will" life into her frail body. Then I chastised myself. Maybe the effort was selfish. Who was I to judge? Maybe God needed her to come "home." Still, I couldn't imagine how anyone needed her more than her children and grandchildren.

That's basically all that happened that first night. I know it sounds anti-climactic. Readers might have expected something more miraculous after such a desperate journey. But the primary miracle had been fulfilled—I'd found Mom alive and breathing. Any other miracle seemed wholly unnecessary.

However, more miracles were about to unfold.

CHAPTER FOUR

Mom

All My Love,
Always and Forever.
—Mary Lou Gurr Asay

*I*t was a twenty-minute drive to my parents' house where I would stay the night. The exhaustion pressed down on me like a grand piano. It wasn't the house I grew up in, but it stood right next door—a smaller, more modern home that my parents built after most of the kids had moved out. Only part of me seemed to be driving my rental car while the other half of my spirit sifted through the images and memories of my life, especially those associated with Mom.

She often shared stories of her childhood in Caliente, Nevada, where her family lived when she was a small child. Caliente is one of those beautiful little towns that few people ever see anymore because of that vast, cold endeavor known as the interstate highway system. Caliente reminded me a bit of Radiator Springs in the animated movie *Cars*. It was a railroad town whose "boom" years coincided with the success and demise of the American railroad.

To this day, many classic buildings are still intact on Main Street, giving it an Old West Americana-type feeling. My mom's father worked as the sheriff of Caliente. If that conjures images of cowboys and old John Wayne movies, it wouldn't be so far off. Mom told us often that her dad's job was "taming all the drunken cowboys that came to town on the weekends."

The stories I liked best were those about her life as a "cave woman." When her family first moved to Nevada, there was "no room at the inn," so to speak, so her family, which included her parents, a sister, and two brothers, lived in a small cave behind one of Caliente's residences. These accommodations were apparently the best available at the time. They lived in this cave two months with no running water or electricity. Her brothers, Bud and Dean, slept in a small camping trailer outside the cave. Presumably the cave had two double beds. With all of today's modern conveniences, the idea of living in a cave for eight weeks still fills me with wonder. How would they have cooked or done laundry? Unfortunately, the questions that occur to me today didn't occur to me as a child, so I never asked. I just liked to imagine my mother dressed up like Wilma Flintstone.

"Momma kept that floor swept so clean." Mom boasted. "You could have eaten right off the (stone) floor!"

Mom said that after two months they moved into a spacious two-bedroom apartment. It was like a motel room with an adjoining door. Talking about this apartment caused Mom's eyes to sparkle because it provided her family with the rare luxury of two bathrooms! It also had two kitchens. However, in 1936, when Mom was seven years old, she experienced something truly terrifying. Late one night someone began pounding on their front door.

"Flash flood!" a voice shouted. "Everybody get out!"

Mom was already asleep when Grandma's voice shouted, "Mary Lou, get up! Get out of that bed! We've got to get out of here! There's a flood!"

Flash floods were frequent in Caliente, Nevada. Caliente's history from its founding in the late 1800s until the 1950s is rife with references to this natural disaster. In this case, my mother got up quickly and fought to reach higher ground. She said "the water was clear up to my chest!" before the family reached safety.

Many homes were destroyed, including the apartment Mom so loved. All that her family had left after the flood was the clothing on their backs. Of course, the Red Cross was there, handing out clean clothes, food, coffee and—oddly enough—plenty of cigarettes. Funny how the world has changed; I couldn't imagine people in modern times donating to a charity so it could provide cigarettes to flood victims. As it turned out, many refugees in Caliente were Mormons who, as my mother liked to explain, "had no use for either the coffee or the cigarettes."

After five years in another apartment, the family finally moved into a permanent home built by my grandfather and uncles.

Mom's childhood home in Caliente, NV
- built by her dad and two brothers.

Then a terrible tragedy struck.

"I was only fourteen when my daddy died," Mom told us, always with a faraway look in her eyes that conveyed deep pain. "Bleeding ulcers . . . the doctors said they could operate and make him well again, but he refused, thinking he would never survive such an operation. He never left the hospital, and two days after his forty-sixth birthday, he passed away. I was the last person that he smiled at."

Shortly after her father's death, Mom moved to Utah with my grandmother where, following high school, she worked as a waitress at a café and later as a telephone operator.

She dated a variety of men. Then she met my dad, the love of her life—Clifton W. Asay. At first she wasn't that impressed.

"My mother fell in love with Cliff before I ever did," she explained.

Mom was seventeen and Dad was nineteen, fresh back from his service in the Merchant Marines.

Dad asked her to prom, but Mom turned him down at first because she knew she'd have to work at the café. However, Dad knew the café's owners, so he arrived one day

Mary Lou Gurr   Clifton W. Asay

during Mom's shift and asked, "Can Mary Lou go to the prom with me?"

"Yes, she can go," her boss replied. "We can get someone else to cover for her."

On the day of the dance, she was late arriving home after her shift and wasn't yet ready when Dad arrived in a car with another couple. Mom tried to tell him to go on to the dance without her and she'd catch up, but Dad patiently waited in the foyer, insisting that he wasn't going anywhere without her. As she got ready, the friend who was still outside with his date honked the horn repeatedly. Dad was unruffled. He told the other boy, "Okay, you found out the horn works. Now try your lights."

That was the night my mother fell in love with my father. He treated her like a princess; he was a perfect gentlemen, generous and sweet. According to Mom, they "danced and danced and danced."

They were in love, but they didn't get married right away. Dad told her that he was leaving to serve a two-year mission for his church in Alberta, Canada. According to my mother, after he made this announcement, without the least hesitation, she promised him that she would await his return.

She wrote to him faithfully every week for the next two years. Shortly after his return, in fulfillment of their dreams, they were married in St. George, Utah, and honeymooned in Las Vegas. The car broke down at one point and it took all their remaining funds to get it running again. They spent the remainder of their honeymoon camping under the stars in Zion National Park in southern Utah. They returned home utterly penniless.

Dad said that as they approached their house, the car was running on fumes. The tank was bone dry as they rolled

Clifton & Mary Lou Asay
Wedding Day - 1949

down the last block toward their driveway. The car had just enough momentum to coast into the driveway and sputter to a stop.

It wasn't long before they started their family, which in time became a whopping tribe of nine children culminating in the birth of my youngest sibling, a sister, who was born on the night of my high school graduation.

Oh, how Mom loved every one of us! Being the second-born and the oldest son, I held an important position of household seniority, which basically meant I got to wash and dry more dishes, mow the lawn more often, and take care of more household chores than any other sibling, with the exception of my older sister, Becky. It was a lot of responsibility, and I'm grateful for the value of hard work which was instilled in me by my parents.

More memories swirled in my head as my rental car and I arrived in the small town of Pleasant Grove. This was where I grew up. My favorite hamburger hangout, the Purple Turtle, was still there, and surely still mixing up the best milkshakes in the world. I passed my childhood home, which had been renovated and refurbished by the new owners. I pulled into the driveway of the smaller house my parents built on the lot next door.

Before I climbed out of the car I peered back at our old house. Lights shone in the windows of rooms now inhabited by another family. Tall pine trees graced the property. The lawn, although plenty big, wasn't as huge as it had seemed when I was a boy pushing a hand mower across it. It was an odd feeling, realizing that someone else was now occupying those rooms. But time, as the saying goes, flows on like a river.

After I left for college, I never returned to live in that house. Shortly after I left, my parents built the new house on the adjacent lot. Though it was always a pleasure to visit, the new house never quite felt like home.

I used the key my father had given me and entered the front door. I was surrounded by familiar photographs, knick knacks, and furniture. I let these memories encompass and embrace me. A couple of old letters on the couch caught my eye—two love letters from my mother to my father. Dad had obviously dug them out during a brief respite from the hospital where he rarely left Mom's side.

My Dearest Sweetheart,

Almost thirty years since our first date, and thirty years being my Sweetheart. Thank you for all you have given me—your patience—your love—nine beautiful children and a life of happiness because I knew you loved me. I love you too Darling with all my heart and every part of me. I thank the Lord every day for you and ask His choicest blessings to be with you, that your leg may heal and not hurt you and you may rest—because you work hard and I know you are tired. I love you and hope you will always Be My Valentine.

All My Love,
Always and Forever,
Mary Lou

My emotions were close to the surface as I reached for a second letter.

My dearest Sweetheart, Clifton,

   I can't begin to tell you how much I love you. You have been so patient and loving to me. I am the most blessed woman in the world, and thank you for all the things you do for me. You are my love, my husband, and my sweetheart. Without you, I wouldn't, I couldn't go on living. You have done everything you could to make me happy and comfortable. Please take care of yourself as good as you are taking care of me. I love you so very much, forever and eternally.

                                          Mary Lou

As I sat in silence, exhausted to the bone, my tears flowed freely. I held those letters in my hands, a physical embodiment of the bonds my parents felt for each other. I thought of the feelings that had provoked my poor father to pull out such letters in the first place. Holding the letters in my hand, I tried to absorb the sentiment in every stroke of my mother's pen. There in the dim light of an old lamp on my mother's old end table, I faded off to sleep.

CHAPTER FIVE

The Miracle

A miracle isn't always
the miracle we're hoping for:
But that doesn't make it any less of a miracle.
—Hana Haatainen Caye

When I arrived at the hospital the next morning, there was little change in Mom's condition. As the day wore on, more family members and friends arrived. Before long, our gathering spilled out into the hallway. The nurses had to decide whether to kick us all out or move Mom to a larger room. Thankfully, they opted for the latter.

My brothers, Randy and Larry, arrived and added their strength of spirit. Larry had brought his guitar and started playing some of Mom's favorite songs. Our whole entourage began singing with him, creating a heartwarming, emotional experience.

"It would be perfect," I remember thinking, "if only Mom was well enough to join in."

On the third day, Mom wasn't responding to anyone. Her doctor and nurses couldn't seem to rouse her. She'd lapsed into a coma-like state, the reality of which pressed heavily on us all. The doctors kept us up-to-date, but none of them gave us much hope. We were thrown into that dismal and exhausting game of waiting. Hour after hour dragged on. There was little to alleviate the sad, helpless boredom. My brothers, sisters, and I crowded around my mother's bed in five or six separate chairs. Despite the heaviness of emotion, we engaged in small talk. Larry and Randy both worked with me in Atlanta and late that afternoon we were discussing the nuts and bolts of our jobs, circumstances with clients, and how to approach various problems.

Suddenly, with absolutely no hint that our mother had pulled out of her coma or recovered to any degree, she sat up in her bed. Her green eyes glistened with the same energy I remembered as a child. With hardly a skip in beat between our trivial conversation and her springing to life, she delightedly declared, "Oh, I have five beautiful sons!"

My siblings and I looked at one another in consternation. Mom looked radiant, even stunning, as if this whole trip to the hospital—the last three days of our lives—had been a bizarre practical joke and she was perfectly healthy and strong. Our exhilaration was intensified by her bewildering words: "*Five* beautiful sons."

My sister, Becky, helped settle her down, propping pillows behind her back. Obviously concerned that she was suffering a spell of dementia, Becky gently reminded her, "Mom, you have four sons, not five. You have five *daughters*."

A smile climbed Mom's face that I'll never forget. If it was possible, her eyes became more radiant than before. She corrected Becky matter-of-factly, "No, I have five beautiful sons."

Last family photo - 1982, I am third on the top row

Dad leaned forward in his chair, his expression just as puzzled as the rest of us. He took her hand. "Well, sweetheart, we have David, Randy, Larry, and Chris. Those are our four sons." With a twinge of hesitation, either because he felt the question was silly or because he had no desire to embarrass his wife, he asked, "Who is the fifth?"

"Shawn," she replied.

Tears welled up in her eyes as she repeated, simply and candidly, "His name is Shawn."

"Shawn?" Dad repeated.

"Yes, Shawn."

My father was glancing around the room, as if asking for some kind of assistance. I think he wanted us to remind him of somebody in our lives named Shawn—a person who'd obviously made a huge and positive impression— someone whom his wife had mistakenly identified as her son. The fact was, there was no one by that name who fit this description. Mom was clearly out of her coma now, but it seemed certain she was still in a state of confusion, although purely by appearance, she seemed as lucid as anyone else in the room.

"I saw him," she continued. "There in heaven. Shawn was there."

We were nonplussed. Some of us might have had our mouths hanging open.

And then Mom's eyes turned to my sister, Connie. She said to her, "Your son, Michael, was there also."

Connie caught her breath. Finally, here was a name that at least some in the room recognized. Precious Michael was the child who'd died in Connie's womb at seven months. The tragedy had occurred a decade earlier, on the very same day as Grandma Flossie's funeral—my grandmother on my father's side.

"Michael?" Connie asked tearfully.

"Yes, Michael, my grandson," Mom replied.

Her tone continued to be so matter-of-fact, as if she was speaking about any other grandchild. We were all silent for a long moment, trying to grasp the significance.

"We know about Michael," someone in the room said. "But who is Shawn?"

"Shawn is the baby Dad and I lost about six months into my pregnancy. I never knew his name until today, and . . ."

As Mom spoke, trying to explain what she had experienced, she seemed to grow very tired. Her words slurred. Gradually, she slipped back into a coma-like state. We all stood unmoving, unsure how to interpret what had just occurred or what to do about it.

When I was fairly certain Mom wouldn't reawaken anytime soon, I decided to head back to the house and get some rest. Before I left, one of my brothers pulled me aside. "What was that all about? Do we have a brother named Shawn?"

I had no reply. I shrugged my shoulders and exchanged confused glances with Dad and several others as I exited the room. Sighing, I stepped onto the empty elevator and pushed the button. Weariness enveloped me. I realized that I wanted to escape into a dream world of my own.

CHAPTER SIX

Revelations

Before I formed thee in the belly I knew thee;
and before thou camest forth out of the womb I sanctified thee,
and I ordained thee a prophet unto the nations.
—Jeremiah 1:5

*A*s I drove back to my parents' home, I pondered what I'd just witnessed. My mother had just reported a near-death experience—there was no other explanation. Obviously this had occurred while she was in a comatose state. She'd met a son who'd died in her womb when he was six months old. This baby had never taken a single breath of air in this life. His name, curiously, was Shawn.

In addition, Mom had met a grandson who'd also been stillborn. Just the thought that my mother was part of that elite—and somewhat controversial—group of individuals who claimed to have passed beyond death's veil and returned to tell about it was astonishing enough. The idea that she'd met two souls who'd never really lived—at least not in the way we generally think of life—was not only astonishing—it was incomprehensible.

I was the second oldest child in my family, and yet I didn't have *any* memory of Mom losing a child. Dad later confirmed that indeed they *did* lose an unborn fifth son between my brother, Chris, and my sister, Suzanne. It had occurred at about the six-month mark of her pregnancy. My older sister, Becky, admitted to recalling the event, but even for her the memory was vague since it was rarely or never discussed.

I pondered about how the loss of a child, after having carried him six months inside her womb, must have affected my mother. Actually, how it would have affected *both* my parents. Mom and Dad loved their children so much—losing even one of us must have been indescribable. To my mother, especially, it would have been devastating. I felt sure that if my parents had given this stillborn child a name like Shawn, I'd have heard about him. A name somehow transforms someone in our minds into a real person, a living soul.

I've always been a bit of an archeology buff; I've visited many of the Aztec and Mayan ruins in Mexico and Central America. If I understood it correctly, I'd learned that among these ancient peoples, children weren't given a name until they were eight or nine years old. This was because the child mortality rate was so high. It wasn't until a child reached eight or nine that a family felt reasonably sure that a child would survive. Perhaps they felt giving them a name would make the pain of loss that much more visceral.

"So," I wondered, "had someone in *heaven* named him Shawn? And why?"

The most exhilarating idea was that a stillborn child should be in heaven at *all*. I'd grown up in a society where prior to birth a child was hardly considered a human being. I was a religious person with strong Christian beliefs. Such convictions, I believe, naturally make a person averse to the idea of abortion. Still, I felt this was a *personal* conviction. I wasn't the kind to carry a sign or enlist in some "movement" to force my belief onto others.

Even so, I'd never before had a specific or logical reason for my belief that abortion was wrong. It was just gut instinct. Something about the sanctity of life—the idea that if a fetus had the *potential* to become a living person, putting an end to that potential was somehow wrong and immoral. Beyond that simple instinct and emotion, I honestly hadn't given the matter a lot of thought.

As I drove toward my parents' house I didn't feel like Mom had given us enough information to really sink our teeth into—just a few brief sentences. Because I knew my mother so well, I believed she'd spoken in a state of perfect coherency, but I also realized that the information was scanty enough that others might interpret it as dementia. I wanted more details, yet we were all very aware that Mom might not live long enough to elaborate upon her experience in "heaven" or tell us anything further about Shawn and Michael.

My thoughts turned to my mother's tenderness of soul. I couldn't help but empathize with her endurance of the loss of a child. How long did she mourn her stillborn son? Why had she never spoken of him to any of us? Why had Dad never mentioned it? Had they forgotten about it until today?

"Of course not," I said aloud as I sat at a stoplight. The mother I knew would never have forgotten one of her children—not even for a moment.

What mother would?

I knew of others, including my wife's sister, who'd lost a child just hours after giving birth. I thought about my own daughter who had miscarried more than once. I remembered the pain and near-inconsolable grief in these women's eyes. On several occasions, I'd noticed an unusual expression of body language—the way they would wrap their empty arms tightly around themselves. The sight tore at my heart, and yet I still felt incapable of grasping the depth of emotions they experienced. After all, I was a man. And perhaps men could not fully comprehend a woman's grief after such an experience. They can certainly comprehend *after* a child is born. A father's attachment can be practically immediate—just as he holds a baby in his arms. But prior to birth, the idea is a little more abstract. Not so for a woman. For some women, I think an attachment for a child is as strong the instant it's confirmed that there is, indeed, a living soul in their womb, as it ever is throughout this child's life.

As I approached my parents' neighborhood, it struck me that my mother's experience of meeting Shawn offered the possibility of incredible hope and comfort to other women who'd walked the same path she had walked. The message was clear—even for parents who lose a child prior to its earthly birth, a joyous reunion awaits in the life to come.

Like shedding a raincoat after the sun breaks through the clouds, I felt my weariness slipping away. I couldn't wait to hear more about my mother's amazing journey. The epiphany I'd just experienced was directly related to a gift my father had given to my mother long ago.

Apparently, shortly after the stillbirth, Dad gave Mom a male life-sized baby doll. I remember sort of scratching my head about this at the time. Why would a husband give his wife—someone who already had multiple children—a "pretend" baby? As a young boy I couldn't possibly have grasped its purpose. I thought Mom might have loved that doll as much as she loved the rest of us. I distinctly remembered petty feelings of jealousy. Tears of guilt welled up in my eyes as I thought about my short-sighted selfishness.

My sister, Becky, recalled how crushing it had been for my mother to simply turn over her baby's tiny body to the hospital personnel. Becky felt sure that this rather cold, informal ending to her pregnancy had haunted Mom for years and left a terrible longing. How had my father known that something as simple as a doll would, in essence, serve as an emotional surrogate for Mom's stillborn child?

Mom frequently held the doll and cuddled it tenderly. If my memory is correct, she sometimes talked to the doll like a real person. I never thought this behavior was abnormal because, in every other way, Mom kept up her usual responsibilities as a Mom.

My father passed away in 2009. Most of my memories of him are of how hard he worked, sometimes holding down three jobs at a time to care for his family. He wasn't a man of many hobbies. He was a jack-of-all-trades when it came to fixing things—even complex electrical and mechanical devices. But in those days such a talent was born out of necessity and not really a hobby. Those who can't afford to hire others will learn how to fix things for themselves. If Dad had any particular hobby, it was his family and the intense love and respect he felt for my mom. If any of us children ever back-talked Mom or showed her any form of disrespect, we knew we'd catch hellfire from Dad. So I suppose I shouldn't have been surprised at his wisdom and foresight, knowing that something as simple as a doll would function so effectively in the way Dad had in mind.

Eventually, Mom gave the doll to my mentally handicapped sister, Collette. Collette's story is very interesting in its own right. It might seem off the subject, but this seems as good a time as any to tell it.

Collette was born on November 19, 1963. My mother was convinced the doctor had counted wrong and that the due date was October 10. This meant my sister may have been inside the womb more than five weeks longer than she should have been. Labor was induced and she was born posterior. The placenta and everything else inside the womb that might support a baby had rotted. Collette had swallowed some and was poisoned by it. She would not cry after she was born and experienced a terrible convulsion. She was transferred to a larger hospital and had passed away by the time the ambulance arrived. Mouth-to-mouth, heart massage, and other techniques were employed to restore the newborn's breathing. Two more times during that first night she quit breathing and had to be resuscitated.

At this time all my siblings and I had gathered at home while Mom and Dad remained at the hospital. My grandmother came to our house to be with us and support us. At Grandma's behest, our family that night engaged in a unique vigil. All those who were old enough starting fasting. That is, we denied ourselves food and water as a means of sacrifice to incur the blessings of heaven. Every half hour, we gathered as a family to pray for Collette's survival and well-being. They said if she lived forty-eight hours she had a 50/50 chance of surviving, but her convulsions were continuous and hard.

Still at the hospital, my mother felt a deep sense of depression and hopelessness. She could not bring herself to pray. In her room she tried to distract her mind by reading a magazine—anything to take her mind off the horrible distress. My mother said that it was while she was sitting there alone that someone called her name: "Mary Lou?"

She looked up from her magazine. "What?"

No one answered.

She returned her attention to the magazine. Moments later, she again heard the voice: "Mary Lou."

She arose and looked around, finding no one. The voice spoke a third time: "Mary Lou, do you want this baby or do you not?"

Mom broke down and started crying. "Yes!" she declared with all her heart. "I want my baby!"

From that moment forward, the depression lifted and my mother was able to pray alone and with my father and other members of the family. As she reported, she could finally "feel something." Later that day the doctor stopped in to see her and reported that Collette was miraculously doing better. He expressed his opinion that Mom's tough little daughter was going to make it.

Collette did indeed survive, but not without long-term effects. Despite her mental handicaps, she has always been a joy and a blessing to our family. There have been many physical trials, convulsions, and seizures, etc. that continually beset her. I remember that she had many bad falls that caused everyone serious concern. But my mother and the whole family always felt that she had "special protection", as if throughout her life a contingent of angels was specifically assigned to her safety and well-being.

Some might wonder why my mother would so passionately inform God (presuming His voice was the voice she heard) that she desperately wanted her baby, Collette. We all knew from the beginning that Collette would face many handicaps and physical challenges, but none of that mattered to my mother. This was *her child*. God had given Collette to her and, as the saying goes, God did not make mistakes. My mother might have chosen to tell that voice that her infant was free to pass through to the next world and avoid the pains she would certainly endure. My mother did not.

It's a sad observation, but in today's world, I think too many mothers would have chosen the latter. They would not have wanted the "inconvenience" of a handicapped child in their lives. But my personal belief is that such individuals come into this world as a means by which *we* are judged. In God's eyes, I believe these individuals are innocent and perfect. It's how we treat *them*, how we care for them, how we sacrifice for them—how we *love* them—that in the eyes of God will have special meaning in the eternities.

Collette with the doll that Dad gave to Mom after the stillbirth of Shawn

Years later, after my mother received the surrogate doll from my father to comfort her over the loss of her infant son, and after Mom overcame her emotional need for that doll, it must have seemed that there was no one in this world more appropriate to receive the doll than my dear sister, Collette. She named the doll "Chris" after my youngest brother, and she has that doll to this day.

As I pulled into my parents' driveway I realized that I, too, felt a weird brotherly kinship to that doll. I wished that through the years, I had known that it was a surrogate for a brother I never knew existed.

As I reached my destination, I felt a sense of contentment. More contentment than I'd probably felt in years.

CHAPTER SEVEN

Me and Wunkin

*You know you're in love when
you can't fall asleep because
reality is finally better than your dreams.*
—Dr Seuss

That night, as I slept in a downstairs bedroom of my parents' home, I woke up shaking and weeping. It seemed strange, considering that my spirits had been so buoyant the night before as I contemplated the miracle of Mother's visit with Shawn. Now I was an emotional basket case—just like so many other nights for the last seven years.

What had awakened me were images and memories of the torment that had afflicted my family. I can hardly talk about it even now. The events had definitely broken something inside me—the very thing that made me so fragile and lachrymose. Because of that fragility, I'll likely offer as few details as possible—just enough to help others to understand the pain and how it relates so inextricably to my mother's miracle. The last thing I'd want is to distract from the extraordinary comfort of Mom's near-death experience and the joy it had brought to her and the rest of my siblings, particularly my sister, Connie, who'd just had it confirmed that her son, Michael, awaited her beyond the veil.

As I think about it, there's only one thing that can crush a parent more than losing a young child. In a practical sense, there *is* no worse pain. *A woman who loses a husband is called a widow, a man who loses his wife is called a widower, and a child who loses his/her parents is called an orphan, but there is no word in the English language for a parent who loses a child (Jay Neugeboren).* An inability to express this grief has gripped humankind since the beginning of time. As a Christian, and as a person who inherited from his mother a deep love for each of his children, I can attest that there *is* one thing worse than losing a young child. And that's losing a child's *soul.*

I'm surely not alone among those who have lost sleep, patience, hair, and mental stability, or simply been deeply, deeply saddened by the choices that one or more of our children have made. As a parent, my heart is bound up in, and dependent upon, the happiness and success of each child more than my *own* happiness or success.

In truth, I don't feel my own qualities as a person nearly match up with my parents. Especially my mother. I'm not saying Mom didn't have flaws. She sometimes gossiped. She could be judgmental and expressed her opinions too openly so that it hurt a loved one's feelings. But other than that, I'm hard-pressed to list any other faults, at least from my perspective.

Maybe it's just that generational thing—the qualities inherent in those that Tom Brokaw coined as the "greatest generation" of Americans. My father was also part of that generation. Their values were just *different* from the values of so many people today. I know young people don't like to hear such things. They feel that those who point out this phenomenon are living with rose-colored glasses. Nevertheless, I believe it's true.

My parents were not prone to profanity. They believed in clean living, serving in their church, and helping their neighbors. They valued self-reliance and abhorred the idea of welfare and consuming more than they needed. When a parent or another family member became elderly, this person generally wasn't placed in a nursing home. We cared for them until death with the attitude that we were performing for them many of the same care-giving functions that they'd performed for us as infants. The people of my parents' generation were generous and kind, did not fear responsibility, and no government agency had to teach them such values. It was a part of their character— an *inseparable* part. More than anything, my parents knew how to sacrifice.

I'm not saying no one today possesses such values. And I'm not saying that those of my parents' generation did not have faults. They did. But something has definitely changed. Now and then, a popular movie or television series portrays the people of the twentieth century as being equally promiscuous, equally profane, and equally callous and selfish as the modern generation. My experience, however, after having lived with my parents and personally observed so many others from that period of history, is that it just isn't true.

My parents' generation smoked more—*that* may be true. Civil rights still had to come into its own. Other examples can undoubtedly be found to contradict the point I'm making, just as examples can be found of people today who are no less stalwart and noble as those of the generation of my parents. However, in general, I don't think this basic reality can be denied.

My parents worked incredibly hard to give their children everything, often sacrificing what they might have given themselves. I'm sure my mother would have liked to have joined various social clubs and enjoyed other activities in the community. She would have loved to travel and see the world. Instead, she gave everything to her kids—time, money, energy, attention, and love. How different this seems from the world of today.

I've been fortunate in my life to have been blessed by two living angels. The first was my mother, and the second is Wunkin. As I mentioned in the preface, Wunkin is my wife, Pam. This term of endearment developed very early in our courtship, sort of a combination of "the One" and "Pumpkin."

I consider my own love story an enduring classic. We grew up only two and half blocks from each other. We discussed it after we were married and it seemed ironic that we'd lived our entire lives side by side. We went to the same church, attended the same school, knew all the same haunts, and had many of the same acquaintances. Still, we didn't know each other at all. Maybe it was just because I was a year older. A year is often a lifetime of difference for adolescents.

We finally met while rehearsing for a church dance. I was seventeen and she was sixteen. My partner was a girl named Debra, who was also my cousin. She and Pam were actually good friends. Pam's partner was a boy who I knew liked her a lot. It was a square dance, so we rehearsed in the same square. In such a dance performers frequently change partners. I soon found that I looked forward to switching from Debra to Pam to execute each motion of swinging her around, allemande left, and do-si-do. Before we finished rehearsing I had the strong impression that Pam enjoyed switching to be with me as much as I enjoyed being with her. In time we'd finagled a permanent change. My primary partner for the dance became Pam.

At this time, we were both committed to attend a Valentine's Day dance with different people. A day before the dance, we both called our dates and cancelled. We then skipped the event altogether and went to a movie—*Bullitt* with Steve McQueen. That night, we fell in love and pretty much became inseparable.

After finishing high school, I went to one year of college. I then did my basic training and advanced training with the National Guard.

Me and Wunkin
Our Wedding Photo
1970

Through all these months while we were forced apart, Pam—my Wunkin—remained admirably loyal.

I never officially proposed marriage to my wife—a fact that she teasingly reminds me of from time to time. Our wedding was just assumed (at least by me).

It was inevitable and expected, so we made all the necessary plans. After our marriage, we moved into an apartment in the Avenues just above downtown Salt Lake City. Our living quarters were about the size of a walk-in closet, but it was plenty big for us.

I never did go back to college. Instead, I found myself working for a wholesale jeweler. I soon looked for a better opportunity and seemed to have found my niche in sales. In a very short period of time, I was earning enough money to provide sufficiently for my family. A couple of years later, we built a beautiful home in Bountiful, Utah, where Pam gave birth to our first son. Two years later, our oldest daughter arrived. Over the next several years, with many up-and-down adventures and several different moves from city to city, we added three more children to our family.

In 1988 I had a job offer from the 3M Company and moved to Atlanta where I became the southeast manager for their mall advertising division. There likely isn't a single shopping mall between Virginia and Alabama that I haven't visited. However, traveling week after week became difficult over time, especially for my wife, who was home alone coping with five growing children. Loneliness on the road was also taking its toll on me. After about two years living in Atlanta, I went to work for a shipping company and was soon able to purchase my own franchise. Owning this franchise and having the blessing of competent and faithful employees gave me the opportunity to be at home every night with my family. This, I now feel certain, was the Lord's way of providing us with sufficient income and flexibility to deal with the dreadful trials that would soon engulf our lives.

This is a period of my life I'd much rather forget. It took great persuasion for me to write any details at all. Then I thought again about the title of this book and the sacred themes I wanted so badly to communicate. I thought about the trials that so *many* parents of this generation have endured. It may be that few have undergone trials that compare to the horror of what we endured. Then again, perhaps few have experienced the miracle of what my mother revealed to us that day in the hospital. I have more details and further miracles to unveil about that experience, but first I felt I should cover, to a limited extent, the details of what happened to my family to provide the appropriate balance.

Both of these events, side by side, express the most powerful message that I can imagine about the eternal and enduring nature of families—the idea that a child, even a child who is conceived, but does not survive long enough to be born into this world, has a literal and indestructible connection to his or her parents. Not only this, but the reality that an infinitely compassionate God can heal a family from even the most devastating events and circumstances. The "catch" is that the family who endures such trials must be willing to reach out and *accept* this healing, even if that road is excruciatingly long and difficult. It seems that often before we can embrace the extraordinary comfort that will invariably be delivered to us, we are forced to endure the most extraordinary pain.

These were precisely the circumstances that were about to befall my family.

CHAPTER EIGHT

The Trial

God asks no man whether he will accept life.
That is not the choice. You must take it.
The only question is how.
—Henry Ward Beecher

*I*t began three and a half years after our move to Atlanta—in 1991. Let me be more specific. In 1991, Pam and I started to become *aware* of a situation that had actually commenced a number of years earlier. It hurts even now, many years after the fact, that I was so oblivious to events as they were transpiring. After all, I was the head of our home! I still grieve that I should have known what was going on. I *should* have known. But I did not, and I have to live with this fact every day. The truth is that my wife and I had no hint of what was really happening until the day she received a phone call from a guidance counselor at our son's high school.

"Mrs. Asay?" began the counselor.

"This is she," my wife replied.

"We'd like to request that you and your husband come to the school tomorrow to meet with myself and the principal."

"All right," Pam said nervously. "What's this about?"

"It's about your son, Robert. He's been suspended and should not come to school tomorrow."

My wife's heart dropped like a stone. Robert was a senior at his high school. We'd known that he was having difficulties—in school, in life, and with friends. He seemed to have socially withdrawn from just about everyone—most of all, his family. He'd adopted the habits of listening to heavy metal rock music, dressing in sloppy attire, and keeping himself generally unkempt. We'd hoped it was just a phase of adolescence—something he would soon outgrow. We were about to discover that it was something much more serious.

Pam and I arrived at the school the following day. The high school principal and guidance counselor sat us down and informed us of some peculiar and disturbing things in which Robert had become involved. They began to reveal, one by one, some very crude writings our son had produced and some highly violent images he had drawn. These writings and drawings had so alarmed and frightened his teachers that we were informed that Robert would be suspended from school. What we were shown also alarmed and frightened us.

Right away, we tried to confront Robert and get to the bottom of this, but he continued with implacable stubbornness to shut us out.

"I don't want to talk about it!" he yelled. "Just leave me alone!"

For the life of us, we could not find a way to break through the wall he had built to insulate himself. By degrees, it became clear to Pam and me that we were embroiled in a situation that neither of us could understand or control.

We tried to seek help for our son. We placed him in therapy with highly qualified psychiatrists. In spite of these efforts, Robert made two serious and heartbreaking attempts at suicide by overdosing on whatever medications he could find. Each time, he was rushed to Northside Hospital in Atlanta where he endured an agonizing stomach pump procedure. After the initial medical attention, they would then admit my child, my flesh and blood, to the psych ward—the *psych* ward!—where men and women wore white jackets and embossed badges with indecipherable letters dangling after their names. They would examine my son for mental illnesses that science sometimes could not adequately define, and at times, it seemed, could not cure.

One night after we brought him home from the psych ward, he bee-lined to his bedroom. We heard the bolt of the door and realized he'd locked himself inside. He then cranked up his heavy metal music to an intolerable level. After a few minutes, we began to hear pounding on the walls. The pounding was relentless and seemed to last for hours. Then the sound changed. I realized he'd broken through the drywall. His next task, I presumed, was to continue destroying his bedroom and break through the next wall into the back stairwell of our home.

I climbed the stairs, determined to stop him, restrain him, do whatever it took to settle him down. I jimmied the lock, but as I tried to enter, I was met by the most violent physical altercation I've ever had in my life. Robert began using vicious profanity and said the most despicable, disturbing things I'd ever had spoken to me—yelling foul threats at the top of his lungs so Pam and his siblings could hear every word. He began shoving me backwards.

"Leave!" he shouted. "Leave me alone!"

This behavior soon transformed into full-on punching with his fists. I found myself forced to punch back to protect myself, protect my family, and potentially protect Robert from harming himself. The more we fought, the harder he laughed—a horrendous, demonic kind of laughter I really can't describe. This was the first time that I felt that my son was literally possessed by something evil, something he had brought into our home.

That night I sought help from the leaders of our church. The pastor of my congregation aided as we restrained Robert inside my home office throughout the night. My son had gone off the rails. It was clear that this situation had become dangerous to everyone involved. I began making many phone calls and other hasty arrangements. By now, Robert was exhausted from the previous night's activities and resigned to what was now happening. At last, we drove Robert, carefully watched and guarded, to the Atlanta airport and flew with him to a psych facility in Bountiful, Utah.

At this point, we still had no idea what had caused this behavior in our child. Pam and I were distraught, flummoxed, and so entirely ignorant of what we had done as parents to provoke this behavior. Or if we didn't directly cause it, what had we missed that had allowed Robert to slip away into such an abyss of self-destruction? We prayed that this facility in Utah, an institution that had been highly recommended by an exceptionally renowned therapist who also agreed to treat Robert while at the facility, would finally be able to reach our son.

The plan was for a thirty-day visit—maximum. Our instructions were to engage in very little contact for the next several weeks. Near the thirty-day mark the facility called me and asked me to fly out to Utah. I fully anticipated that I was going there to fetch Robert and bring him home—a new, enlightened, and healed individual. As soon as I arrived at the facility, I was brought into an office with a panel of therapists. The doctors immediately asked if my wife was with me.

"No," I admitted. "I'm sorry. That wasn't really practical. Pam is home taking care of our other children."

The therapists became deeply concerned. Apparently there had been some kind of miscommunication. I realized that their instructions that Pam fly out with me were more than a suggestion.

"Mr. Asay," one of the doctors said, "before we can get into any further details of what we've learned about Robert, your wife—Robert's mother—should be here. She should be sitting at your side."

The seriousness settled in. The very next day, Pam made arrangements for the care of our children and hopped on a plane. Waiting for my wife made for one of the longest days I can recall. The facility had deliberately left me in the dark. My imagination went into overdrive. What had I missed? What horrible thing had taken possession of our son's spirit and life? And how had such a thing been allowed to occur?

I greeted Pam at the airport and we immediately drove to the institution. As we sat together before the same panel of therapists, I was stunned to realize how limited their information was—how little they had actually learned.

"Whatever is going on with Robert," the doctor told us, "it's going to take much longer than just thirty days to get it resolved."

"I don't understand," I said. "He's been here for a month! Does it normally take this long?"

"In a case like this, the answer is often yes. The hurts, the events, that have placed Robert in this frame of mind are very serious and very deep. There's no schedule. No ticking clock. Getting to the bottom of it will take as long as it takes."

"All right," my wife said. "We understand. So how long can he come home with us before we have to send him back?"

"Mrs. Asay," said the doctor, "we cannot recommend that Robert leave this facility. We advise that you and your husband go home. We will provide regular updates on everything that we learn as we learn it. If we don't continue the therapy—uninterrupted—we have no doubt that Robert will continue to be a danger to himself and to others."

My wife was in tears. "Can we see him?" she asked.

It was near the end of our visit that Robert was finally brought into the room. His face was beaming with joy and relief, which only tore at our hearts because Pam and I knew that he had every expectation that we had come to take him home. He embraced us both simultaneously.

"I love you!" he said. "Thank you! Thank you for coming! Let's go home!"

I wasn't going to draw this out. He had to know what was about to happen.

"We love you too, Robert. We love you so much. That's why we can't take you home. Not yet."

I saw the panic enter every part of his body. His eyes widened and welled with tears. "You can't leave me here. You *can't!*"

Pam was in tears, but she knew she had to be supportive of what I had said. "We *have* to, Robert. The doctors tell us you're not ready. We want you to come home so badly. But we want you to come home the right way. Happy. Healthy . . ."

"No!" he wailed. "I want to go home. You have to take me home! Please don't leave me in this place!"

His mental state was rapidly deteriorating before our eyes. He embraced us again, only this time he was determined not to let go. Hospital personnel had to intervene to peel him away. He wailed as he was taken forcibly from the room. My wife hid her face in my shoulder and both of us wept deeply and bitterly, not caring that we were still surrounded by doctors and therapists. We'd flown all the way from Atlanta to Utah, and yet the total amount of time we'd spent with our fragile son was less than ten minutes. To this day, Pam and I will both declare that leaving Robert at that facility and flying home to Georgia was one of the hardest things we've ever done.

We did as the doctors had recommended. We abandoned our son (or so it felt) for an undefined amount of time at a psychiatric hospital almost two thousand miles from home. Perhaps it will be no surprise that immediately after we departed, Robert was placed on suicide watch for several days.

Over the next few weeks and months, we would receive frequent phone calls from the facility, asking questions and updating us on the latest information that had been revealed by Robert. It was very much like peeling the layers of an onion, only this onion had layers seemingly reinforced by impenetrable steel. Our son remained at this facility for nearly a year.

In bits and pieces, snatches and revelations, my wife and I learned that our son had been ritually and sexually molested beginning at the age of five. Such abuse had been perpetrated by people we knew very well and had trusted. I have committed not to reveal in this book who these people are. If I did, the poignant and tragic nature of this event would be considerably heightened. Let it be known, however, that I did not withhold the perpetrators' identities for *their* sake. I did it for the sake of others, and that's as much as I'll ever publicly reveal.

Suffice it to say that the abusers were devout servants of the occult. The abuse that had taken place actually occurred before we'd ever moved to Atlanta. Pam and I sincerely did not have a clue that any of this was happening. We'd obliviously given over the care of our children into the hands of a very dangerous and destructive resource on countless occasions while they were very young. The only hint I had that something dark and ominous was taking place was when I walked into the basement of a home where these individuals were staying and found the walls, the floors, the bed, and every other area of the room littered with images of hardcore pornography and occultist paraphernalia. This event occurred after we'd already moved to Atlanta, but prior to Robert's melt-down and prior to learning any details of what our son had experienced.

The perpetrators had ritually ingrained a sinister warning into our son's mind that if he ever divulged any portion of what had been done to him, he and his family would suffer a painful and horrible death. The reality of this poisonous threat was a pivotal piece of the puzzle for our own understanding of what was going on. It was the only explanation that helped us to fathom how we'd been kept in an utter state of ignorance for so long. It also explained why it took so long for psychiatrists and therapists to peel away the complicated layers of falsehood and deceit.

We presume that this ritualistic abuse of our son continued until he was about thirteen years old, or until we left the area. We later learned that during those abusive years, prior to our move to Atlanta, Robert had been carefully trained and manipulated to sneak out of our home in the middle of the night. This had apparently occurred on numerous occasions. His abusers would be parked just up the street, waiting for him. He would then be transported someplace where these occultists would conduct their unspeakable rites, twisting and warping our child's mind, forcing him to endure a world of torture and debauchery that would undoubtedly affect him for the rest of his mortal life. Suffice it to say that for Pam and me, this was a nightmare beyond our comprehension or imagination, and the beginning of countless hours of therapy sessions for our entire family.

And still the pain was far from over. While he was still incarcerated at the facility in Bountiful, Utah, Robert became involved in a work release program. He accepted a job in a field he loved—electronics—working for a friend of mine who lived in a nearby town called Farmington. He soon had his eighteenth birthday and remained at the institution. However, after a few more months he became aware that the facility could no longer hold him without his legal consent. Almost immediately, Robert discharged himself. This was wholly against his doctors' recommendations, but Robert had convinced himself that he was ready to take the world by the horns. He moved in with a friend he'd met at the institution with the eventual plan that he would return to Atlanta. At this time we were informed by authorities, and *he* was informed, that even if he moved back to Atlanta, he could not move back into our family home or be around his brothers and sisters.

Robert found a car—an old VW Beetle Baja. I purchased it to provide him with transportation to and from work. For a time, he seemed to be doing okay. His performance on the job began to slip and he was told that he would no longer be able to work at the electronics firm owned by my friend. He made his decision to move back to Atlanta.

We made arrangements for him to stay with some friends of ours in Roswell, Georgia. This couple did not have any children. During this time, my wife and I installed a high-end security system for our home and property. It was not purchased for the usual reason that most might have to install a security system, i.e., to protect our home from intruders or burglars. Instead—and my heart aches to admit it—it was put in specifically to protect our family from Robert.

It's critical to understand that we simply did not fully grasp what was happening with our son. We had no personal knowledge of the kinds of demons (figurative and literal) that were constantly laying siege to his mind and soul. We sincerely feared he might be inclined—perhaps beyond his control—to harm his parents or one of his siblings. Even if our paranoia was a bit over-the-top, we felt compelled to do everything possible to protect our home and family.

"Dad," Robert announced one day as he called me in Atlanta from his domicile in Utah, "I'd like to come home. I think it's time."

I drew a deep breath, feeling both relief and trepidation. How was it possible for a father to feel both of these emotions simultaneously? I loved my son and I wanted him close, but we remained terrified that his treatment and recovery were far from complete.

"All right, Robert," I told him. "I'll fly out to Utah and we can drive back to Atlanta together."

"Really, Dad? You'd do that with me? Er, *for* me?"

"I wouldn't have it any other way."

Robert had interpreted my offer as a desire to spend time with him, and he wasn't wrong. But honestly, I had a more important motivation. Something inside me whispered that if I didn't help my son make this two-thousand-mile drive home, he would never arrive. At least, not alive.

A week or two later, I flew out to join up with Robert and prepare for our epic road trip to Atlanta. Randy, another dear friend of ours who lived in the Salt Lake area, couldn't bear the thought of me cooped up in a tiny VW Beetle with my son and all his belongings.

I guess I should make another confession. Before all these challenges regarding our son, I'd never had much of a problem with weight. However, the daily stress of the last several years had, like other fallible human beings, enticed me to turn to food as a major source of comfort and solace. I regret to say that during this period, I'd stacked on over 100 pounds.

I had a feeling that my recent weight gain was part of the reason why Randy made Robert an incredible offer. Randy was kind of an automobile buff and loved to collect and fix classic cars.

"Robert," Randy said to my son, "have I ever told you how much I love that VW Beetle of yours?"

"No, Randy," Robert said. "You haven't."

"They're becoming mighty rare," he went on. "Sand dunes."

"What?" Robert asked.

"The Little Sahara and other dunes in Utah. Ever heard of 'em?"

"Maybe," said Robert. "My dad might have taken us there when I was a kid. Renting 4-wheelers."

"4-wheelers!" Randy brushed this off as a truly inferior way to experience the glory of these magical mountains of sand. "There's no factory car in the world better suited to joy-riding up and down those dunes than a VW Beetle Baja. They make the best sandrails. Right now, you happen to be the only person I know who owns one. What would you say to the idea that you and I swap straight across—your Beetle for my Saab."

My jaw practically hit the floor of his garage. Randy's beautiful Saab 900 was parked just outside, covered up by a winter tarp. Randy had shown it to me before. I knew it was used, but there wasn't a scratch on it. The interior was immaculate. I had no doubt that this Saab was worth ten times the value of Robert's Beetle.

"Randy," I said, "thank you, but . . . I just wouldn't feel right. I mean, I don't think such a trade would be fair."

Randy frowned, but there was a twinkle in his eye. He clicked the inside of his cheek. "You gentlemen drive a hard bargain. I'll tell you what. If you'd like, I'll throw in some extra cash for the trade. Will that make it fair? What do you say? Do we have a deal?"

I suddenly understood what Randy was doing. His gesture of kindness was so selfless, so generous, that there are no words to adequately express my appreciation even to this day. Randy had decided he wasn't going to take no for an answer, and Robert suddenly found himself the proud owner of a Saab 900.

Not long after that, Robert and I embarked on our two-thousand-mile escapade from Utah to Georgia in the dead of winter. I did my best to chart a southern route with the expectation of fairer weather and safer roads. This route would take us through northern New Mexico, across Texas, and eventually into Atlanta.

The first leg of our journey, driving from Salt Lake City to Price, and southward through Moab, Monticello and Cortez, Colorado, was rather uneventful. That is, uneventful except for a screaming blizzard and a blinding snowstorm that practically frayed every last nerve in my mind and body by the time we finally rolled up to our motel in Gallup, New Mexico.

We gratefully spent the night in our warm motel room. The next morning, the sun was brilliant and shining. However, there was still a blanket of snow on the ground, and plows had only been moderately successful at removing this hazard from Interstate 40. Our intent was to work our way eastward to I-20 and then down through Dallas.

"Dad," said Robert, "when do you think I'll get a chance to drive my new car?"

It was easy to forget that it was *his* new car. Up until now, I'd been doing all the driving. I sensed his impatience. A nervous feeling coiled in my guts, but I relented and said, "All right. At the next exit, we'll pull over and I'll give you a turn."

"There's an exit just ahead," he said eagerly.

He'd apparently seen the highway sign even if I didn't. Why did I feel so nervous? He had a license. He had driving experience. It was only natural that he should have a chance to drive his own car. I was aware that he was still taking medications, but I really didn't think any of them would entail side effects that would interfere with his driving.

"Okay, partner," I said, pulling off the highway a mile later. "The wheel is yours."

The roads by now were fairly clear, but there were still patches of black ice and snow. Now seated in the Saab's passenger seat, I felt compelled to offer Robert some stern instructions. "Remember, son. Don't drive too fast. And keep your eyes peeled for ice. If you're going to do the driving, you have to be very, very careful."

"You worry too much, Dad," was his wry response.

At first, everything seemed well and good as his driving remained relatively safe for several miles, yet I found it impossible to shake my nervousness. I noticed that the speedometer was steadily edging higher. A few minutes later that speed—and his overconfidence—began to surge. I found myself holding onto whatever I could with an increasingly tighter grip until my knuckles were white.

"Robert, you need to slow down," I warned.

His eyes were fixed forward. I couldn't tell if he was concentrating or if his thoughts were zoned out. Whatever the case, he was not heeding my advice.

Robert began to pass other vehicles, cutting sharply in front of them as he switched lanes. My nervousness had reached the breaking point.

As forcefully as I could muster, I said, "Robert, if you can't drive safely, I need to take over."

Again, this statement didn't register. I didn't know if his mind was clouded with medications or if it was something else.

"Robert!" I said. "*Robert!*"

His eyes looked glazed over, as if my son wasn't even there. He was driving dangerously fast. If the highway hadn't been perfectly straight, the wheels would never have been able to grip the road. I saw a road sign that indicated a rest area just ahead.

"Robert, take the next exit. I mean it! You *will take the next exit.*"

Somehow this message got through. He knew I wasn't taking no for an answer. Reluctantly, and without a word, he began to approach the off ramp.

"Robert, press the brakes! You're still going too fast!"

Was he angry at me? Did he have a death wish? The Saab was on a direct collision course with other vehicles at the rest stop. At the last possible minute, Robert hit the brakes, but he hit them too hard. The vehicle began to skid off the roadway to the right. It was obvious that our car could not avoid sliding off the pavement. We did so with a bone-shaking crunch and wallop. The car dropped about seven or eight feet and landed on its side in a gully filled with massive boulders. With the driver's-side wheels of the Saab directed skyward, Robert and I were snugly entangled on the passenger side of the vehicle.

To escape we were forced to crawl out through the driver's-side door. The accident had shaken us both to the core, but fortunately neither of us was seriously hurt. Admittedly, I was steaming inside. Mostly I was disgusted with myself for allowing Robert to drive in such adverse conditions, and also in his current state of mind, which was nowhere near stable.

I called Pam and told her what had happened. The very next phone call I made was to Randy in Utah—my friend who'd swapped us for his beautiful Saab. Now for the frosting the cake—Randy informed me that he'd already removed the vehicle from his insurance. Additionally, I had yet to call my *own* insurance agent to have the vehicle added. The Saab was a total loss.

Well, let me amend that. It wasn't a *total* loss. After a tow truck finally arrived at our remote location, it managed to pull us from the rocky gulch and tip the vehicle back onto four wheels. Miraculously, the thing was still drivable. It was conspicuously dented and out of alignment, and there were major gaps in the passenger side doors. Still, I felt our best option was to continue our journey to Atlanta in this less-than-desirable condition. A chilling wind whistled through the passenger-side door for the duration of our road trip, but after countless miserable hours, we managed to hobble into the driveway of my Atlanta home.

Afterwards, we put in place some arrangements I'd made with our friends in Georgia. He had a room where he could stay, but the unwavering instruction from therapists and doctors was that Robert should not be allowed, under any circumstances, to live inside our house. He stayed with this couple for a while and started looking for a job.

Shortly afterwards, and again for reasons that were never fully divulged to Pam and me, this couple asked our son to leave. For a while, he was forced to live in his broken down car. He would often spend the night inside his car in a local park or Walmart parking lot, but he didn't feel safe and didn't sleep well. He then asked us if he could park in our driveway. It was a long horseshoe drive with a thick cluster of trees in the middle and provided some privacy from the street so he would feel safe enough to sleep. It's impossible to describe our feelings of distress and sadness. Pam and I wept together in our bedroom many nights knowing that our son was outside in our driveway, shivering under a blanket. Sometimes, the following morning, if he was still parked there and after our other children had left for school, we would invite him inside for something to eat.

Robert started working here and there and living with a girlfriend in an apartment about thirty minutes away in Sandy Springs, Georgia. Over time, we only saw or heard from him about once per week, and by all outward appearances he seemed to be getting by. However, it was soon evident that he was becoming more and more anxious and uptight. Something was happening inside his head. It had to do with his twenty-first birthday, but we weren't quite certain what it meant. His mother and I watched him sinking into a deeper and deeper depression.

He would often come to the house for some first aid help from his mother. It seemed he'd deliberately cut on both his arms. Sometimes there would be dozens of deep razor cuts from his shoulder to the bottom of his arm just above his hands. His arms and shirt would literally be drenched in blood. Pam would wash him up and apply medication and bandages. On more than one occasion, his girlfriend had to rush him to the hospital emergency room because he'd cut himself so badly, he needed stitches.

This was highly upsetting to his family and everyone else. We called to talk to his doctors about what was going on and were told that it was a form of psychological release from anxiety, pressure, and depression, but that it was not done as a suicide attempt in any way. We desperately tried to persuade him to continue with therapy, but he was not interested and there was little we could do but watch, wait, and hope things got better.

We learned that part of the brainwashing he had endured since he was five years old was that he would not live beyond his twenty-first birthday. This, he felt, was something over which he had no control. He was just supposed to die, whether by suicide, getting hit by a truck, or some other method that would end in a fatal result. We entreated him with every shred of logic, every argument we could devise, to convince him that it simply wasn't true, but Robert continued to believe he was destined to die.

As the inevitable day drew nearer, our son started coming apart at the emotional seams. Pam and I were convinced that if no other options presented themselves, he would feel compelled to take his own life. We felt powerless and desperate. And it goes without saying that we didn't want this to happen anywhere in the vicinity of our other children.

The day before his twenty-first birthday, Robert was an utter basket case, hardly able to communicate. I convinced him to go with me on a father-and-son excursion to Panama City Beach, Florida. Not knowing what he might do, I had rented a home on a favorite golf course to give us plenty of privacy and isolation. I sat awake with him through all the darkest hours.

"You'll be all right," I assured him. "Everything will be all right."

Robert continued shaking uncontrollably, intermittently breaking into tears. "You don't understand," he said to me. "Nobody understands!"

"I understand," I said. "You're afraid. And that's okay. I'm your father. I'm here. And I'm not going anywhere."

"It's not enough," he insisted. "You can't stop it. I'm going to die, Dad. And there's nothing anyone can do about it."

I embraced my son. "That's a lie, Robert. You're safe. Nothing can hurt you here. Nothing can get to you. You'll see. You'll see."

He continued to weep and shake his head. The hours on the clock seemed to tick by so slowly. We never fell asleep, and very little more was said between us. I kept this arduous vigil with Robert until the sun finally crept up over the horizon.

A sense of overwhelming relief, celebration, and rejoicing overcame us as those bright crimson rays broke through the clouds and Robert realized that he had survived. He was still breathing. We tightly embraced with tears of joy streaming down our faces. For the first time throughout this entire ordeal that had besieged him since he was five years old, my son slowly began to reject all the lies that had permeated his mind. He was finally starting to recognize the difference between truth and light as opposed to manipulation and brainwashing.

Throughout this ordeal, I realized I'd learned an incredible lesson. It's a lesson I'm not sure many parents have the opportunity to learn. Sometimes a father (or mother) is asked how far they will go, what they will sacrifice, and how much they will endure to save the life and soul of their child. I learned that there are few, if any, limits that I wouldn't have exceeded or barriers that I wouldn't have broken down to accomplish that objective. I realized that I loved my son—just as I love every other member of my family—with a fist-clenching passion that compares with no other drive in my life.

And perhaps, because of it, I understood a little more about the emotions felt by a Father and His Son that night in a small garden called Gethsemane. It was here that a lone

Child begged His Eternal Father to spare Him the indescribable pain He was about to endure. I think that this Father would have done anything possible to spare His Son the trauma that was about to befall Him. I cannot fathom the emotions of a perfect Man begging His Eternal Father to "remove this cup" from Him, "if it was possible."

At that moment, even the God of us all wondered if there might be another way. If there *had* been another way, I have no doubt that His all-loving Father would have spared Him the agony. The fact was, there *was* no other way. What had to be done, *had* to be done. The Atonement, the salvation of you and me and the family of man, *had* to be accomplished. So the ever-humble, trusting Son finally assented, saying to His Father, "Thy will be done."

I am by no means a perfect father, and I would do anything to correct my mistakes. If there was one event I could change—one thing I could go back and erase from my family history—it would be to go back and rescue that five-year-old boy from the unspeakable years of horror and abuse. My son was a precious, innocent soul who'd been dragged through a mire of evil that I pray very few human beings will ever know. What happened to him was something he could not control. He was just too young to defend against it. And the course upon which it set him became something fixed and unrelenting.

Please don't misunderstand. The last thing I would want to do is offer up some kind of undeserved defense of my child. Nevertheless, I sternly proclaim my belief that the full accountability for the domino effect of what occurred will not be felt by Robert. It will be felt by his perpetrators. And I thank God that I am not saddled with the responsibility of making those final judgments. Such judgments will be left in the hands of a perfect Being and they will be incontrovertibly just.

If God would permit it, I'm quite certain I would give up my own life to go back in time and fix that singular terrible wrong. But God hasn't yet provided us with that kind of time machine. I'm sure, if He had wanted, God could have spared my son the awful experiences he endured. For some reason, God did not spare him. So the question remains, what will my son and the rest of us do with that reality? How will we let it affect us? What can we do, and what *will* we do, to allow such events to shape our souls for what awaits us in the eternities? All I can hope is that the efforts I have made to heal those awful scars will be viewed by my Maker as sufficient. I hope it will be viewed as equal to the love I feel—and the love I *gained*—for my precious son. Also the love I gained for my wife, my other children, and for my fellow human beings on this fast-spinning world.

After his twenty-first birthday my son's demeanor began to change. The evil that had afflicted him since early childhood started to fade and disperse. His countenance brightened and he managed to find a good job—one that allowed him to pursue his love of mechanics. He was hired by a national chain in their automotive department. Eventually he was introduced to the woman who would become his wife. It wasn't long after meeting that these two became like peas in a pod. Or, as the line made famous by Forrest Gump states, like "peas and carrots." They fell in love and soon were married and living like a couple of hippies, enjoying the same music and clothing and taking life in stride.

Her arrival in his life at this particular period was a miracle all by itself, and certainly an answer to many prayers. My son still faces challenges, issues of anger and depression, as well as other hurdles, but his wife, Tricia, is a genuine blessing to his life and she holds his hand through the rough patches with incredible patience and love.

After a few years, Robert attended diesel mechanics school, and to this day, he works for a local truck dealer. Considering that we never thought he could ever again be happy, that he'd ever be married, or could ever hold a steady job, we consider every single day an extraordinary blessing.

Our family will never fully recover from this horrible chapter in our lives. I'm not sure that we're *meant* to. What we endured is now a part of us. But there can be no doubt that the timing of our mother's experience in the hospital was profoundly appropriate to help me and Pam put into perspective the eternal nature of our trials and, of course, the eternal knowledge that all the sacrifices we make to help our children and help each other are *never* wasted. Such actions, even those that seem petty or fruitless, have eternal ramifications. Each sacrifice forges eternal relationships that cannot be broken—even by the bonds of death.

This was the lesson I learned from my mother and from my son. And, although I haven't met him yet, I know that this was also the message delivered to us by my unborn brother, Shawn.

CHAPTER NINE

Good-byes?

Good-byes make you think.
They make you realize what you've had, what you've lost,
and what you've taken for granted.
—Unknown

I'd been in Provo, Utah, now for several days, visiting my
mother at the hospital. I was home now, resting on my
parents' sofa. I ran a towel through my wet hair. The hot
shower I'd just taken felt good and had relaxed me. It was
early evening. I was about to read the local paper when the
phone rang. I hardly dared to move.

"Dave, you need to get back here," my sister Becky said
on the other end.

"What's going on?"

"Mom's awake. And Dave . . . she's saying . . ." Her voice
broke. "She's saying her good-byes to everyone."

I drove to the hospital in record time. Rushing to my
mother's bedside, I took her hand and leaned in to kiss her.
Her eyes opened ever so slightly.

"Oh, David, I love you." Her voice was barely a whisper.

"I love you, too, Mom." I hadn't even expressed my final good-bye before she lapsed back into unconsciousness—the coma that seemed determined to take her from us. I looked around the room at my family. Everyone was quietly weeping, fearing that this was "it."

Mom's doctor came into the room and confirmed what no one wanted to hear—it was unlikely she'd make it through the night. I looked at my father, who'd been here at his wife's bedside night after night. He appeared as red-eyed and ragged as I'd ever seen him.

"Dad," I said, "why don't you go home and try to get some rest? I'll stay with Mom and call you if anything changes."

"I hate to leave her," he replied.

But he reluctantly agreed to go home for a while. Two of my sisters had been with Mom since the day before, so they too departed along with the rest of the family. This allowed me to spend some precious alone time with the woman whose sparkling green eyes never failed to light up a room. I prayed silently for those eyes to open just one more time.

As I sat in the chair by Mom's bed, holding her hand, I felt somehow comforted by her steady, labored breathing. The night wore on and I started reminiscing about other late nights when Mom and I had shared so many stories at the kitchen table. Before long, I started to doze off. I was awakened by the squeeze of her hand. It was four o'clock in the morning. Mom was awake and alert.

"I love you, David," she said. "I love all my children. Do you know how lucky I am to be married to your father? I can't tell you how much I love that man."

Her mind and speech were as clear as the day she'd sat up in the hospital bed—as lucid as any other time in recent memory. For a full forty minutes, we talked about everything and yet nothing of particular importance. Finally, she drifted back into a normal state of slumber.

A nurse entered the room around six o'clock. Mom awoke as the nurse tended to her needs. Family members started filing in an hour or so later. They were pleasantly surprised to find Mom not only alive and awake, but with her vital signs steadily improving.

Over the next few days, she continued to improve. None of us could believe it. We'd all prepared ourselves emotionally for Mom's death. Considering the internal roller coaster we'd all put ourselves through, this development, while welcome and full of relief, was a strange twist of fate. Life can be an inexplicable thing. And I have no doubt that our Heavenly Father has an uncanny sense of humor.

Soon the doctors agreed that it was time for Mom to be discharged. She still required a great deal of care, so it was decided that she should be transported to a nearby nursing facility. I decided to fly home to Atlanta to tend to my own family and ease somewhat back into my normal life.

"I'll be back in a couple of weeks," I told my sweet mom as I was leaving.

Her visit to the next life and her reunion with her fifth son had been temporarily set aside, but it would soon be revisited as I and other family members anxiously sought additional details.

CHAPTER TEN

Implications

Life can be seen through your eyes,
but is not fully appreciated
until it is seen through your heart.
—Mary Xavier

*I*t seemed sooner than expected that I found myself back at the Atlanta airport, gripping my carry-on bag as I walked outside into the passenger pick-up area where Pam was waiting. After our usual greetings and expressions of love, Pam began the drive home.

"Okay," said Pam. "I'm all ears."

"Where do you want me to begin?" I asked.

"From the beginning. I'm ready to hear all the details about Mom's 'visit', now that you've had time to think about it."

I told Pam all I remembered about Mom's near-death experience, my newly revealed brother named Shawn and my newly discovered nephew named Michael.

As I concluded my account, Pam insisted, "You need to record Mom's experience so our children and grandchildren will know."

"I know," I said. "I'm already planning that, honey, but . . . you know how I can be. Thanks for the reminder, and I'll probably need a couple more."

"You may even want to consider writing a book," Pam suggested.

The idea threw me for a loop. I'd never written a book before.

"Mom's certainly not the first person to have a near-death experience," I said. "What would be unique about any book I might add to the stack?"

"The implications," she replied.

"What do you mean?"

"I agree," Pam began, "that hundreds, perhaps thousands, of people have had a near-death experience. But this one had the aspect of a baby who died as a stillborn, yet apparently still exists just like you or me, only in a different realm. A *higher* realm. They're not just a wandering angel in heaven, but a part of our family. *That's* the story you need to tell. Shawn and Michael are real people still connected to *us*. Consider the hope—the comfort—that such a message could provide. Think of all the lives of aborted children that might be saved."

I squirmed in my seat. "I don't know if I want to be a mascot for that kind of message. Ultimately, this would be a religious story. And I've never been much of a preacher."

Pam was undaunted. "It doesn't matter if it's religious or just a story about life after death. It just needs to be honest. Then people can decide for themselves."

I had a flash of all our family's trials and felt overcome. "Who'd want to hear a story like that from us? Think about what our family has been through. If I was truly honest, I'd have to be honest about *everything*."

"So why not?" Pam said. "What makes us so different from other people who've endured awful hardships? Maybe that's another thing that would make this book unique. Don't forget that this experience happened to us. To *you*. Your mother reported this miracle for your benefit and the benefit of all her posterity. Other members of our extended family have endured difficult trials. I think the majority of people on this earth endure such things! Maybe not exactly like ours, but they can relate. Oh, I promise they can relate.

"Some people might think a near-death experience—even by a close family member—only happens to people who are particularly special—somehow favored. One book I read was about a preacher—a man of God—with a young child who'd had such an experience. Another was about a man who'd undertaken special projects to serve his community all of his life. If these authors had ever endured genuinely gut-wrenching trials—I mean beyond the *physical* trials that brought about their near-death experience—they didn't mention it in their books. The message of *your* book would be that God loves us all, even those whose imperfections are legion, whose struggles are less physical and more spiritual in nature. I'm talking about true earthly suffering that relates to this generation.

"Moreover, the message of your book would be that God loves not only our children who die young or die in the womb, but that He loves those who live to an age where they can utterly break our hearts. He *does* love them, David—our children who struggle. He loves them more than we could ever imagine. More than we love them ourselves. This book should be about comfort. Comfort for mothers. Comfort for fathers. Comfort for children. Comfort for families."

Still feeling uncertain, I replied, "I'll commit to writing about it in my journal. Honestly, I think there's more to learn. Mom is still very lucid and alert. She's never provided the full details of what happened that day in the hospital." I heaved a heavy sigh. "I can't say that I feel comfortable yet writing a whole book. We'll just have to see what happens."

Pam smiled lovingly. "I'll take that as a good beginning."

CHAPTER ELEVEN

The Special Visit

Death…is no more than passing from one room into another.
But there's a difference for me, you know.
Because in that other room I shall be able to see.
—Helen Keller

I returned to Utah two weeks later. However, I entered the nursing home only to find my mother's room empty.

"Excuse me," I said to the first nurse I could find. "I'm Mary Lou Asay's son, and I was just in her room." The concern in my voice was evident, but the nurse smiled warmly.

"Don't worry. Your mother's just down the hall with her physical therapist." She gave me directions to the physical therapy room.

"How's she doing?" I asked.

"Oh, she's doing quite well. It's mostly the diabetes bothering her now. It causes pain in her legs and feet. We're trying to relieve some of that. She's such a delight! We really love having her here."

I grinned with the same pride as if she'd said this about one of my children. Mom's beautiful eyes lit up when I entered the room.

"This is my son, David," she gushed to her therapist.

"Another one?" he said, seeming surprised. "How many children do you have?"

She replied, "I have nine beautiful children."

"Or ten, depending on who you ask," I casually added, thinking Mom might have no memory of her special "visit."

"That's right," Mom quickly reaffirmed. "I do have ten."

The therapist looked puzzled.

Finally, I asked, "Mom, do you remember what you told us in the hospital . . . about . . . you know . . . your fifth son?"

Her face brightened. She looked right at me and tearfully replied, "Oh, yes, I remember everything."

I was stunned and relieved. I'd braced myself for the possibility that Mom might have forgotten her visit to heaven, even if it really happened, especially in her present condition. Her affirmation was so nonchalant, yet startling; you could have knocked me over with a feather. Not only did she remember, but she remembered *vividly*. I asked if she'd mind if we talked about it. I added, "I mean, are you *comfortable* talking about it?"

"Of course I am, David."

I could hardly wait for her to finish her physical therapy session. Questions percolated in my mind. As Mom and I settled back into her room, she asked about Pam and the kids, how things were going with our business, when the rest of the family would be visiting, and so on. I gave short answers, wanting desperately to turn the conversation to the subject I deeply wanted to discuss.

Finally, I leaned forward. "What was it like there? You know, in heaven? Were you inside or outside or . . . ?"

She paused and said thoughtfully, "I'm not really sure. The location changed. At first, we were in a very large, spacious area with lots of people. Hundreds, maybe thousands! They seemed to be meeting or visiting with their loved ones. It was like a huge reception area."

"Did you see anyone you knew?"

"Oh, yes!" Her voice was animated. "My mother and father were both there. As were my sister, your aunt Thelma, also my aunt Marie, and Grandmother Edwards. I also remember my mother's sister, Aunt LaRue. There were other relatives too—so many I just can't name them all."

"Mom, you told us of meeting your fifth son. Do you remember that?"

"Of course," she answered, almost scolding. "Shawn was there."

"Shawn? Is that what you and Dad named him?"

"Oh no. I had a stillbirth. I was about six months along when I lost him. Daddy and I didn't talk about a name for him. It just wasn't done back then. They also didn't bury a stillborn child in those days. We simply donated his body to the hospital." Her eyes grew distant, as if remembering a real, visceral pain.

"So how did you know his name?"

"Well, that's a funny thing," Mom replied. "He just told it to me. I was in the reception area and this tall, handsome young man walked up to me with open arms. He wrapped them around me and gave me a big hug and kiss. He smiled, looked right into my eyes, and said, 'My name is Shawn. I'm the child you lost before birth many years ago, and I love you so very much.'"

My mother continued, "I remember I was so happy. So overwhelmed with happiness to finally meet him. I had no idea that I would be meeting him there. No idea that he even *existed*.

Shawn and Mom - Joyous Reunion

Charcoal sketch by Stephen Stauffer,
made from a photo of Mom
and a description of Shawn provided by Mom.

But there he was. He said he had so much he wanted to learn from me. And then, with such a warm and loving tone in his voice, he thanked me."

"Why did he thank you?" I asked.

"He said, 'I am so grateful for everything you've done for me.' I looked at him rather dumbfounded and said, 'But I haven't done anything for you.' His reply was quick and filled with love." My mother's smile as she described this scene made her look ageless. "'Yes, you have,' Shawn said to me. 'You have done *everything* for me and I love you so much.' He again expressed his love and said he was very thankful for a loving mother and indicated that he was eternally grateful. I simply didn't know what to say. I was overwhelmed."

"It sounds obvious that he was happy to see you."

"Oh, yes! He was very happy to see me! And I was so happy and grateful for the opportunity to meet him and know that he was my son."

I could feel my emotions welling up, but I didn't want this to interfere with my interview, especially since I wanted to soak up every detail. I tried a short question. "How old was he?"

"He appeared to be in his twenties. Actually, he looked quite a bit like your brother, Larry Dean."

"What about your parents, Grandma and Grandpa Gurr? And your sister, Thelma? How did they look?"

"They looked wonderful," she said, smiling. "*Everyone* looked wonderful. They welcomed me with long, warm hugs and kisses."

"How old did they appear? I mean, did they look to be the same age as when they died?"

"Oh, no. They were in their twenties as well. Late twenties, I would say. They looked perfect."

"Then how did you recognize them? I mean, some of these people, like your grandmother and grandfather and Aunt LaRue. You wouldn't have known them in their twenties. Just in their forties, fifties, or even sixties."

"Well, I'd seen pictures, of course, when they were younger. But no—" She became adamant. "No, pictures wouldn't have mattered. I would have recognized them anyway. Don't ask me how. I just knew who all of them were."

I listened in amazement. This conversation was surreal. My mother was never a "storyteller"—never someone to tease me by "pulling my leg" and later report that she was "only kidding." That just wasn't her personality. I'd had many long talks with this extraordinary woman and her voice had the same tone it'd had all my life—the same as if she were telling me what she'd had for supper the night before.

She went on, "Eventually we left the reception area and went to our house. I mean, our *family* house. I'd never seen it before. I suppose it was the home of my grandparents. Maybe it was the home of my parents. It didn't matter. It was *my* house too. It all seemed normal. It belonged to our entire family, and it was very nice. Mother was working in the garden planting flowers— *gorgeous* flowers with varieties and colors I'd never seen before. Thelma was working there too. And there was a lawn. I can't remember what my daddy was doing. I only know that he was there. Shawn was there too, standing in a row with the other boys. I remember that our house was in a kind of neighborhood, but honestly, David, I wasn't overly concerned with the little details. I was just interested in my family."

"What were they wearing? Was everyone dressed in white?"

"No!" She laughed, as if the question was an outdated stereotype. "Everyone just had on regular clothing. My mother and Aunt Thelma wore regular clothes. No wings or angel-white dresses. Still, the clothing was beautiful. *Everything* was so beautiful and radiant. The *colors!* David, there were so many beautiful and bright colors—colors I can't describe. Colors we don't see here. I so look forward to seeing all those colors again."

"Could you move? I mean, were you able to walk?"

"Yes!" Again, she relished the memory. "I was able to walk around and move like I haven't been able to do for many years. It felt so good. It was wonderful, actually."

I continued my barrage of questions. I hadn't written them down beforehand, but maybe I should have. Each question came to me off the top of my head, the same questions that any living soul might have wanted to know.

I asked, "Other than your ability to walk, were you the same as you are now?"

"I was a young woman again—like the others. No more pain. I felt perfect and wonderful and then . . .well, I came back to this." She was referring to the pain-racked, decrepit body she now inhabited, riddled with discomfort. I could sense a pang of regret in her voice.

I hesitated before asking the next question. "Mom, if it was that wonderful, why didn't you want to stay there?"

"I did," she admitted. "And my mother and father . . . and Thelma and Shawn . . . all of them wanted me to stay. I would have done so, too. But I had an *overwhelming* feeling that I had to come back—that there was something very important left for me to do."

I leaned forward. "What?" I asked eagerly.

She paused for a moment, deep in thought. "I'm not sure." She said this with a bit of frustration and disappointment. "I honestly can't remember. I apologized, of course, to many of my loved ones who asked me to stay. But I knew I had to return. I can't say that I regret this decision because I have my whole family here. My husband. My children. My grandchildren. Maybe the reason I came back has something to do with my family. Or with *your* family."

Or with *everyone's* family, I thought, but I didn't voice this idea out loud.

Her eyes looked far away, lost in memories. Then she changed the subject to the mundane, everyday things of life—wondering what they would be serving her for lunch, asking when I was going back to Atlanta, and other topics that are the norm between a mother and son during such a visit. Still, I couldn't help wondering how many human beings had ever had a conversation like the one I'd just enjoyed.

I left my mother that day with deep feelings of gratitude. I thanked God for allowing her to have this experience and to share it with me. Indeed, to share it with all of her family.

And now . . . to share it with you.

CHAPTER TWELVE

Clarity

It is difficult to say what is impossible,
for the dream of yesterday is the hope of today
and the reality of tomorrow.
—Robert H. Goddard

Over the next few days, as life slipped back into a mode that was "normal," my mother's expressions about my brother, Shawn, and my nephew, Michael, were never far from my thoughts. I felt drawn to my sister, Connie, and her experiences losing the child in her womb.

He'd died about seven months into her pregnancy in 1987. On the very day our grandmother had her funeral. Not long before this, we'd lost our dear aunt Thelma to cancer. She'd been like a second mother to us kids. All of those events—happening so close—were nearly more than Connie could bear. She slipped into a state of depression.

This was all a decade before Mom had sat up in her hospital bed to say she'd met Connie's stillborn son.

My mother's stillborn son was never given a name, but Connie had very carefully and thoughtfully selected Michael's name. She and her husband, Floyd, were quite adamant about it. And from the outset, Connie had resolutely believed Michael would be with her in the next life.

Connie had told me that she and Mom had some serious disagreements over her stillborn child. Mom maintained that Michael could *not* be considered a real person. Her reasoning? Connie had not held him in her arms as a breathing baby. *That* was Mom's criteria for what constituted an enduring connection between mother and child. She did not consider it appropriate that Connie and Floyd should give this infant a name. This made it all the more ironic when Mom awakened that day in the hospital to report that she'd actually met Connie's stillborn son. She'd met her grandson, Michael.

I wasn't quite sure why Connie was so unshakable in her conviction that Michael was a real person, though stillborn at seven months. She'd had another miscarriage very early in her marriage at about the four-month mark, and also felt strongly that this child—named Julie—was a real person who awaited her in heaven. My mother had never mentioned meeting Julie during her experience, but I had the strong impression that Mom had only described the tip of the iceberg as far as the details of her visit to heaven, so Julie's existence certainly wasn't implausible. In any case, none of these beliefs were part of any specific Christian or biblical doctrine I'd ever heard, yet Connie had a firm, unyielding conviction about the matter.

Now Connie's mother—*my* mom—who'd fought so hard to convince her to dismiss such nonsense—was the one who'd confirmed that Michael was a real person. I couldn't help but wonder if the depression Mom experienced after her own stillbirth had influenced her efforts to dispel such hopes in the mind of her daughter.

Obviously Mom had fully relinquished any concept that she'd ever meet or know her own stillborn child.

Now everything had flip-flopped. Mom's experience at the hospital had provided all the hope that *both* of them needed to prove that their sons awaited them in the life to come. Even pondering this filled me with wonder and . . . yes, with comfort.

The evening after arriving home in Atlanta after visiting Mom in Utah, I called Connie spur of the moment. I was seeking clarity. I wanted to know her opinion about what Mom had said. It was good to hear her voice when she answered at her home in Wyoming.

"Okay," I said to Connie after the usual greetings, "so we have a new brother in heaven. What now?"

That's all I said at first. I hadn't spoken with Connie one-on-one since that day in the hospital. I wasn't certain of her interpretation of what Mom had said, so I suppose I was fishing.

She replied, "It's not just our brother. Based on Mom's visit to heaven, Shawn and *my* son, Michael, are both alive on the other side."

It was a relief to confirm that she remembered everything exactly as I remembered it.

I said, "If we accept that, it also means that stillborn and miscarried babies—even aborted babies—are actual developing human beings. Just because they die prematurely, or we voluntarily abort them, it doesn't mean they cease to exist."

"It's enlightening," said Connie, "but also somewhat frightening. What if Mom *didn't* really visit heaven? What if she just *thought* she did?"

"You mean, what if Mom imagined it? What if it was all a dream?"

Connie said patiently, "Do you think for a minute that it was a dream?"

"No," I replied. "She was in complete control of her faculties—as clear as you and I right now when she sat up in that hospital bed. I should also tell you, I visited Mom again in the nursing home. Connie, you should hear some of the details of her experiences on the 'other side.' Wonderful things. Some of it you wouldn't believe."

"Oh, I'd believe it," she corrected. "I'd believe it with every fiber of my being. Every member of our family—everyone there at the hospital that day—knew she was telling the truth.

"She'd fought with me so sternly years before when I told her that Michael was a real person. Now she was telling me the opposite. I haven't had a chance to visit with Dad about everything yet, but I think he also believes everything she said."

"I've never personally had an experience that proves life after death," I admitted. "This thing with Mom might be as close as I ever get. I've always believed that our spirits live on after we pass away. But Shawn—his existence—now verifies this. An important mystery, at least for me, is solved."

"And think about it," added Connie. "Shawn and Michael were both premature, stillborn babies. Yet their spirits live. It's time to think about what we should do with this knowledge."

I bit the inside of my cheek. "Let's say I tell this story to my friends. What will they think? What will they think about *me?*"

"Does it matter?"

I thought for several seconds. "No, it really *doesn't*. In my business, I've become good friends with a lot of people—people from many religions and many walks of life. I know if I told this story to some of my friends, they'd think I was nuts, and I don't think some would hesitate to give me that opinion."

"Whatever their religion or perspective," Connie said, "I think this event can help them clarify their own beliefs. I don't care if they're atheist, agnostic, or Confucian. Who cares? Just tell people about Shawn, about Michael, and let them decide for themselves whether to accept it."

My mind was turning quickly. "I have a neighbor, Mrs. Jefferson. She had a stillbirth a few months ago. I wonder what she would think."

"Exactly," said Connie. "Shawn's story could comfort so many people. Potentially every mother and father who've ever lost a baby prematurely—or even in infancy. But Mom's message goes even deeper. It testifies of the bonds of love that exist between family members. Not only in this life, but on the other side of the veil. Those bonds are so much stronger than people realize. Virtually unbreakable. If a stillborn child can thank his mother so sincerely—so profusely—just for giving him life, think of what that means to a parent who raises a child through every phase of childhood and adolescence only to experience the most terrible sorrow, the most heartbreaking of events.

"Think of it, David. Mom's story is about the indomitable nature of families. The eternal connections between parents and children, cousins and uncles, grandparents and great-grandparents, etc., etc. It's like an unbreakable chain, and every link matters. It matters to God. So it should also matter to us. Oh, Dave, I do hope that you end up at least writing a short book. For some, these words could be life-altering."

Again, there was that idea (that may have included a "nudge" from Mom) of writing a book.

Still, for many years I did nothing beyond recording each event in my journal. I'd also read other books about near-death experiences to compare them with my mother's. Admittedly, there were similarities, but also discrepancies, usually minor ones. One mentioned angels with wings, yet my mother was pretty clear that nobody had wings. To my surprise, other authors mentioned that during their near-death experience, they'd met stillborn or miscarried children. One author said she'd met a child who was miscarried at two months old!

While I was doing this research, the daughter of some dear friends miscarried a child. She was broken-hearted and in such pain that I immediately wrote a brief version of Mom's story and gave a copy to my friends. They were deeply moved, and later I received a sincere expression of appreciation from their daughter.

My desire to write a detailed book was steadily building. I just had to put it down in words.

And then shout it from the mountain tops.

CHAPTER THIRTEEN

Unexpected Departure

Death is nothing else but going home to God,
the bond of love will be unbroken
for all eternity.
—Mother Teresa

*D*uring the next several weeks, I flew back and forth between Atlanta and Utah several times to see my mother. Her heavenly visit was never discussed in great detail again. Despite her painful physical state, she seemed intensely happy, yet she never could shake the mild frustration of not being able to remember why it was important to return from heaven to her aged, diseased, and hurting body. The question of "What was I supposed to do?" plagued her often.

One Sunday, when it was almost time for the nursing home's church services to begin, I asked if she'd like me to take her there.

"I think," she said thoughtfully, "that I'd rather stay here and visit with you."

No objection from me. I'd flown all the way from Atlanta. If Mom felt spending her precious, personal time with me was more important than anything else, I was certainly willing to oblige. As we often did, we popped a movie into the VCR in her room and sat together watching it. I even got one of the nurse's aides to fix us some microwave popcorn.

Later, we talked of family and many of life's most important things. I flew home satisfied that we'd had a productive, enjoyable visit, and I had already made plans to fly back again.

My mom during her last days in a nursing facility, holding one of her favorite movies and book.

* * *

A few days after that visit, I called Mom from Atlanta.

"David," she said, "I'm so glad you called. We need to talk about something."

"What's that?" I asked.

"I want you to tell your children and future generations about my visit to heaven. I really was there, and Shawn and Michael really do exist. It's important that they know. Please let all of them know how precious they are and how much I love them. My fervent prayer is that you and all your brothers and sisters will treat each other with love and kindness. Forgive each other of any trespasses. And please, David, know that I love you and your sweet family so much. Promise me you'll do these things."

I was a bit taken aback by her earnestness, but I replied, "I promise I'll do my best. You know I love you."

"Yes, David, I do."

"You know I appreciate all you've done for me."

"Yes."

"Take care, Mom. I'll be back out to see you in a couple of weeks."

We said our good-byes, not knowing it was the last time I'd ever speak with her—at least in this life. She passed away within a couple days of that telephone call, quietly slipping into eternity in the early hours of night with her beloved husband and two of her five daughters by her side.

My sister Becky was holding Mom's hand while Dad dozed off moments before in a nearby chair. Celiene was awake, but her eyes were closed. Becky said she felt the actual sensation of Mom's spirit leaving her body. She sat still a moment before disturbing anyone else, reflecting about what had happened. Losing Mom was not unexpected, but it was difficult nonetheless. Becky wiped away her tears, then alerted Celiene.

But Celiene was already awake. Becky didn't have to tell her that Mom had gone. She knew.

"Becky," she said, "I could smell Grandma Gurr's raisin-oatmeal cookies. Didn't you smell them?"

Grandma Gurr's raisin-oatmeal cookies were legendary in our family. No one else had quite perfected her recipe. Although I wasn't exactly sure why Celiene should smell such an aroma at the instant that Mom slipped away, I believe my grandma was responsible for making that happen from the other side. And for my sisters, it was a tender testimonial that Mom was reuniting forever with those she loved.

At last, my sisters awoke my father to tell him. Dad's eyes filled with tears. He walked over to his sweetheart and gave her a last kiss, expressing his love and reminding her that he would join her in heaven at the appropriate time. They let the nurse know, who asked if they'd like to remain with Mom for a time. Dad said tenderly, but in his familiar, practical tone, "No, she's no longer here. Let's go home."

It goes without saying that I wished I could have been there to say one last time, "I love you, Mom. Tell Shawn hello." At some point, there are no more "one last times."

This was that point.

CHAPTER FOURTEEN

What If?

*It is better to know some of the questions
than all of the answers.*
—James Thurber

*M*om's funeral was a solemn and joyous occasion.
Glowing tributes were paid to her, the music was uplifting,
the floral arrangements heavenly, and love permeated
everything and everybody. I wanted to capture the essence
by bottling up the atmosphere so I could remove the cap
later whenever I needed it to buoy me up.

The next day, Pam and I found ourselves alone at the
cemetery. We stood near the new grave, admiring the
flowers, both silently thinking our individual thoughts
about life, death, heaven, and the prospects of meeting
Mom in the hereafter.

Pam broke the silence. "Did you notice that no speaker
at the funeral mentioned Mom's visit to heaven?"

"I did notice," I replied. "I wonder why we didn't think
to have someone tell that story. I'm not sure very many
people beyond our close family members know about

Shawn and Michael." I felt frustrated as I declared, "Why didn't I think about it?"

"Well, we can't beat ourselves up over it, playing the 'What If?' game."

"The 'What If?' game?"

"For example," Pam continued, "what if Mom had never had her near-death experience?"

"Well, we wouldn't know about Shawn or Michael. We'd merely believe or hope that life goes on after we're six feet under. But she *did* visit heaven. She *did* return to tell us about it. We buried her yesterday, but Mom *is* still very much alive. We *will* know each other again. Unborn babies are *real* people—even when miscarried, stillborn, or lost to abortion."

"Those are *monumental* conclusions. Here's another 'What If?' Pam said. "What if we fail to tell everyone we can about what Mom experienced?"

"I'm not sure. It's not like we can tell the whole world. Besides, the world wouldn't believe us."

Patiently, Pam responded, "We can *try*. If people don't believe us, that's their free choice. If you knew that half of Atlanta would be destroyed next month by tornadoes, wouldn't we try to warn as many people as we could?"

"Of course."

"Well, Shawn's story is even bigger. Millions of people—and notice I said 'people'—lose their lives every year because of miscarriage, stillbirth, and abortion. Shawn and Michael told your mother something important. I think they want us to spread their message."

"Don't you think that everyone who believes in God knows at least something about life after death?"

"At least they *think* they know. The message of Shawn and Michael is, in many ways, entirely unique. If mothers-to-be knew about Shawn, they'd fight with all their strength to protect the unborn. If fathers-to-be knew about Michael, they'd protect them with every ounce of their energy. If medical doctors knew, they might refuse to participate in terminating an unborn baby, unless the mother's life was genuinely in danger."

"A lot of doctors *do* refuse to participate in abortion," I countered.

"I know. But knowing about Shawn would add a *new* reason. A new layer of understanding. They might become more vocal in protection for the unborn."

"Yeah, but if they knew everything about our family history, maybe that perspective would change things a little. Sure, Robert is a success story—at least today. With so many others who emerge from a world of abuse, the story doesn't end in success. It ends in a ruined life. Ruined forever. Some might think it'd have been better if someone like Robert had never been born."

"That's not how our Savior felt," said Pam. "He felt exactly the opposite. And He said for those who offended His 'little ones' it would have been better if the *offenders* had never been born."

"The 'millstone' analogy," I said thoughtfully. "I remember. 'Better for them if they'd been drowned in the depths of the sea.'"

"What about you?" Pam asked. "How do you feel about what happened with Robert?"

"*Me?* I'm the man I am today because of that struggle. I'm not saying it wasn't difficult, excruciating, heart-wrenching, expensive, and that the effects don't trouble us still today. But it's *because* of what I went through with Robert that I truly learned how to love. I think I knew how to love before, but with Robert, God took me to a new dimension that I never knew existed. I wouldn't change that for the world."

"You wouldn't give it back?" Pam asked.

"No, I wouldn't! I mean, I've often moaned, 'Why did this have to happen to us?' I've fretted and raged inside—wishing I could change things, if possible. But return those experiences? If it meant I'd lose Robert forever? Never!"

"How many parents do you think need a message like that?" Pam asked. "It's easy to love a newborn baby. It's easy to relate to such a loss. So simple and pure. It's far more difficult to empathize with what may be the spiritual loss of an older child. We often joke about how we love our babies, we adore our toddlers, but wish we could stick our teenagers in cages until they're adults. Unfortunately, it doesn't work like that." She altered the subject slightly. "I know that a major argument of people who support terminating the life of an unborn child is that too many unborn children are not wanted. They don't have a fighting chance in this world. Nobody loves them. As a result, they're bound to become a burden on society."

"That's ridiculous," I snapped. "*We're* society—you and me. I took on that burden with Robert. Without me and you and our family and so many others who loved him, he wouldn't have made it."

"So what about those who don't have you or me and so many others? There are those who argue that because children *have* no love or support, they should be aborted."

"They're wrong," I said angrily, almost forgetting that I was having a rhetorical conversation with my wife. "The burden is still on us. Society needs to learn how to love just as much as individuals—and the example it needs to learn from is *families*. Think about the gratitude Shawn felt toward Mom, Pam. He thanked her 'for everything she'd done for him.' Yet Mom had no *idea* what she'd done for him. She didn't think she'd done *anything*. Still, he insisted that she'd done 'everything.' We assume he was referring, perhaps, to the opportunity to have a mortal body, although he never said it directly."

"It might go even deeper," Pam added. "Shawn hugged and kissed your mother and considered her part of his intimate family. That connection seemed to mean the universe to him. He *yearned* for that connection. He desperately wanted his mother to stay with him in heaven. Mom felt badly that she *couldn't*, and yet a few months later, she returned to his embrace."

"What about a mother hooked on crack cocaine who deliberately aborts a baby because she's afraid of abnormalities—handicaps? She's also afraid that her addictions will leave her in no position to take care of a baby. Wait, I have an example that might be even *more* selfish. What about a woman who aborts her baby because she fears she's not ready. In some cases, it might even be true, but the idea of putting the child up for adoption doesn't really even cross the woman's mind. She thinks having that child—or even carrying the baby for nine months—will interfere too much with her freedom, her upward mobility, her edge to compete in the marketplace, or it will just make her life more complicated. What kind of connection will remain in the afterlife between *that* mother and child? Would a baby still feel any connection with a mom who deliberately terminated his or her life? Would they feel the same gratitude?"

Pam sighed. "We can't pretend to understand these things. Thankfully, there's a higher power who can judge far more insightfully and perfectly. Think again about Mom's experience in heaven. All of those relatives. Dozens."

"I had the impression there were *hundreds!*" I said. "All of them felt a deep, abiding connection to Mary Lou Gurr Asay."

Pam pondered another angle on the matter. "You said some of them were standing in line to greet her," she reminded me. Shawn said there were things he wanted to 'learn' from Mom. Maybe those are things he could have learned more easily if he'd been born. In any case, it seems like he's going to get a second chance."

"But that doesn't mean we ignore those granted a *first* chance," I replied. "For kids born to mothers or families who don't want them, Mom's visit tells us that there *are* people who *do* want them. Even if they don't live in this realm, they feel a deep and abiding connection to that particular soul that we couldn't possibly comprehend. It might be a grandmother or great-aunt or cousin or an ancestor from hundreds of years ago. If no one else, *God* wants them. He loves them. But I don't think God is ever alone in His feelings. He's just the most powerful link in the eternal chain of the human family."

Pam added, "If the world fully understood these links and that the most important struggles we'll ever face in this life involve our children—fighting to save every one of them—maybe we'd feel committed to never give up that fight. Too many think that achieving success in their careers is most important. Sure, it has its place. But compared to building our families, saving our loved ones, any other accomplishments pale. By comparison, they're actually silly."

I sent her a crooked smile. "And you came up with all this just by playing the 'What If' game?"

"Absolutely. So what if we do nothing with the knowledge that you have a brother named Shawn?"

I shrugged. "Life will go on."

"Sure—just as it has for centuries. But what if we did something to share with others the first words your mother heard when she visited heaven—'My name is Shawn, and I love you so much'?"

I chose my response very carefully. "It's like we've said before—if we can comfort even one distraught mother, or if even one expectant woman chooses life for her child because of what Mom saw, our time and effort will be well spent."

"And don't forget about Robert and the rest of our children. What we gained *because* of that experience. The love we learned through pain."

"Pain that almost killed us," I added, thinking about the stress, weight gain, and other complications.

"I don't think that matters. Well, sure, it *matters*, but little by comparison. Yes, we're better off if we can conquer the challenges that go along with our trials. And it's not too late. Certainly your mom's story by itself can't change the world. But David, it might change somebody. Do you remember the story of the little girl walking along the seashore where thousands of starfish had washed ashore? An elderly gentleman watched her pick up a stranded starfish and gently toss it back into the ocean. He asked, 'Why are you doing that? There are so many. What you're doing won't make any difference.' She tossed another starfish back into the water, looked up at the man, and said, 'It will make a difference to *that* one.'"

"I get your point," I said, "and I suppose you're thinking of the book again. But everything is too close right now. I can't see the forest for the trees."

"That's all right," Pam said. "Let's go home, let time heal a few more of the wounds. But I hope you remember what we discussed today."

"I will," I promised. "I don't think I could forget even if I tried."

CHAPTER FIFTEEN

Ton of Bricks

But what am I?
An infant crying in the night:
An infant crying for the light,
And with no language but a cry.
—Alfred Lord Tennyson

*W*e all know how fast time flies. And we know that life moves on after the death of a loved one. Both of those truisms have impacted me in the years since my mother passed away.

Another truism is the one associated with good intentions—the road to *you-know-where* is paved with them. That reality surfaced quite forcefully in 2010 on the twelfth anniversary of my mother's passing.

I was in a melancholy mood to begin with that day. It seemed to have enveloped me completely as I was contemplating the deaths of my parents—Mom in May of 1998 and Dad in January of 2009. I sat quietly with my journal open before me. Once more, I chided myself that twelve years had passed and I had yet to fulfill my promise. What was it going to take for me to finally get my hind end in gear and write this book? I remained in this state of frustration and exhaustion as my eyes fell shut. My head dropped to my chest. I was soon blissfully asleep sitting at my office desk.

I awoke with a start. For several moments, I had difficulty remembering where I was. As reality came back, I felt a renewed determination. It hit me like a ton of bricks. At long last, I started writing in earnest about my life and the things that have brought me such extraordinary comfort.

I'm now approaching the end of the project. It has been an exhilarating experience. I've shed many tears recalling so many heartwarming and harrowing events. I feel as though I've had numerous reunions with Mom. I also feel like I've come to know my brother Shawn intimately. I feel as though they've spoken to me many times throughout this project and, at times, renewed my feelings of comfort.

I never wanted the politics of abortion to overshadow this story. I just wanted to write a book about Mom, Shawn, Michael, Robert, and the trials and triumphs of my family. However, I can't deny that the implications of abortion are clearly relevant in this story.

Again I said to myself, "If just *one* pregnant woman who is considering abortion reads about Shawn and Michael and changes her mind, *all* my efforts writing this book will have been worth it." It was the same lesson of the story about the little girl and the starfish."

In addition I told myself, "If even one overwrought parent struggling with a wayward child is wondering if all those hours of rocking them to sleep, panicking to get them ready for school, struggling to help them tie their shoelaces, biting nails to the bone waiting for them to come home, and tearing hair out to convince them to make the right choices—if any parent is wondering if those efforts are worth it, I'm here to report—based on my own experience and the experience of my mother—the answer is an unequivocal yes.

"I love you, Mom," I said out loud.

"I love you, David," I clearly heard in the recesses of my mind.

CHAPTER SIXTEEN

Epilogue

*The best way to get to heaven
is to take it with you.*
—Henry Drummond

*M*y mother has been gone from this world for almost sixteen years now. I still miss her terribly. She suffered to give me life and sacrificed to nurture and care for me. She wept for me when I hurt, and I know she always loved me.

I've always felt I knew the reason she came back from her visit to heaven and suffered two more months inside her disease-ridden body, even when she didn't know it herself. It was to give me and other members of her family a special gift and glimpse of what lies ahead, to tell us about Shawn and Michael, and also to strengthen our resolve never to give up on our children, grandchildren, and anyone else who stumbles and needs our help to rise again.

She needed to remind us that if God never gives up on our loved ones, neither should we. For whatever reason, Mom needed to remind us of the unbroken chain of eternity, and the blessing and privilege we have through the grace of Christ to reclaim loved ones we have lost physically and, in many cases, spiritually.

I realize that answers can sometimes create a million more unanswered questions. I'm here to admit that I don't have those answers. I don't know whether or not women who wantonly abort unborn children will have the same privileges of knowing and loving their children as those who lose such children by natural causes. Society has twisted so many of these values to the point that many don't even grasp what's right or wrong. Accountability must be combined with knowledge, so I'm not here to judge. Nevertheless, I *am* convinced that each of us must do our part to *spread* that knowledge—to stop the selfishness and senselessness.

I regret that I've waited so long to get this message out. But maybe that's okay. The intervening years have served to heal my family to a great degree. Time has also provided incredible clarity regarding Mom's spiritual message.

I know that I'll see my mother again, and I'm excited to meet my brother. But honestly, this reunion will mean much less if it does not include my wife, my children, and every other human being I've ever loved.

Because of Mom's detailed description of what happened to her, I know she is, at this moment, happy. She's without pain and able to walk, run, dance, and enjoy being with so many of those who departed this mortal existence ahead of her. Finally, she is enjoying—as only a mother can—getting to know the son she never knew while still in this life. In my mind's eye, I feel I can see her dancing and laughing. And I know Dad is there, taking care of her.

From time to time since Mom's passing, I have felt the warmth of her love wash over me, leaving me with the peace of being forgiven for my shortcomings as her son and as a human being. After all, she is my mother. She'd forgive anything. And so I've been comforted that this same forgiveness will be granted by a much higher authority, my Savior Jesus Christ.

I wanted to express one final thought about my father. Mom had such a great love for him. He cared for her with adoration and uncompromising respect for so many years. I marveled at his patience as he cared for my mentally handicapped sister with such devotion and sacrifice. My dad must have been a financial genius. He provided for a family of nine children on a school custodian's salary. Never did any of us lack for decent clothes or shoes or gifts on Christmas morning. We were never hungry. When the need arose, Dad wouldn't hesitate to take on a second job to make sure we had what we needed. My dad is a wonderful example for me. Perhaps he wasn't perfect, but he was as close to a saint as I'll ever know in this life. His most important lesson was this, and I hope it also becomes the theme of this book—our noblest calling in mortality—and perhaps beyond—is to serve our family. Thinking about it now, my mother's visit to heaven was only confirmation of the example my father had set his entire life.

Dad passed away in 2009, having lived more than a decade without his sweetheart. I can easily imagine their joyous reunion, perhaps in that same beautiful reception area she once described. Never again will my parents be separated.

After Dad's passing, Collette moved in with my brother Randy and his wife, Rosa, who love her dearly and take such good care of her. I am so grateful for the love and secure, happy home they provide for her. She is our very special sister.

I have composed a short farewell letter to my mother, and occasionally I read it to myself in her honor.

My Dearest Mother,

I do love you with all my heart. I appreciate all you have done for me and for all of your children and grandchildren—no mother has ever shown greater love for her family than you have.

Thank you for making the difficult choice to come back to your diseased and hurting body to share your wonderful and sacred experience with your family and such a powerful message of comfort and hope with the world.

I am so happy you are now at peace, without pain, or grief and enjoying this time with Shawn, Michael, Dad, and other loved ones. I look forward to the time when Pam and I, along with each of our children, are reunited with you and Dad and the rest of our loved ones. I have to agree with my brother, Shawn—I am so grateful for everything you have done for me, and I love you so very much.

> *Love,*
> *Your son,*
> *David*

AFTERWORD

by Melissa Ohden

My first reading of Dave Asay's manuscript caused me to experience an almost overpowering feeling of déjà vu in two respects.

First, the primary message of the story is hope, comfort, and anticipation for all mothers and fathers who have experienced the terrible trauma of losing a child by miscarriage or otherwise.

When Dave asked me to read it, he was not aware that I had recently experienced a miscarriage—he was seeking my thoughts from the perspective of an abortion-attempt survivor. *Extraordinary Comfort* touched me deeply as I reflected on the painful loss of my own precious child, and the story of Dave, his mother, and family validated my thinking about life as we know it and about afterlife as we might experience it. I confess that there's more I don't know than I do know about afterlife, but *Extraordinary Comfort* has reinforced dramatically my conviction that I'll be reacquainted with Gabriel, my miscarried son, in the afterlife, where I'll love him much as I would have loved him had I not miscarried.

Second, an underlying message of *Extraordinary Comfort* relates to the feelings we humans will develop if we'll let ourselves reflect adequately upon the consequences of abortion from a pro-life perspective. I'm a living example of a failed abortion that enabled me to live and compelled me to speak out about my biological parents' illogical pro-choice thinking. Yes, I survived a failed saline infusion abortion in 1977 when I was born alive after a gestation period of about seven months. Naturally, I feel like I can speak with a voice of authority when I talk about abortions.

"Every pregnancy is different," people kept reminding me during the initial stages of my second pregnancy. "It must be a boy with the disposition of his father, all laid back and calm, not fiery like his mother," my husband Ryan and I joked. Call it a mother's intuition, but I knew there was something incredibly different between my second pregnancy with Gabriel and my first pregnancy with Olivia. Little did I know that the major difference in my two pregnancies was that the first resulted in a live birth, whereas the second would end tragically in a miscarriage.

I'll be honest—I still lie awake many nights talking to God about why all of this happened, about what His divine plan is for our child's life, for our family, and for our ministry. My heart aches with a grief I never knew existed. The fears and anxieties about life and even death that I first faced years ago—after finding out the truth about being an abortion survivor and spending years working through the consequences—stirred once again in my soul during the first few days of our loss. That's the by-product of experiencing a trauma, of facing a loss—it rocks your foundation; it shakes your core. Yet, despite all the pain, there is something beautiful that rose up from the ashes. There was a transformation happening within me, within our family, that brought me peace and filled my grieving heart with joy.

Even in my times of vulnerability, even in my times of feeling weak and unprepared on this journey, I was being lifted up by God, and so was my entire family. As a woman who felt shattered and broken, I subsequently found an inner strength that is even greater than the one I had known before as an abortion survivor. Like so many other women, I am a woman who has lost a child through miscarriage. It is not something I wanted to experience; but let's be honest, I never was looking to be an abortion survivor, either. Now both are a part of who I am, and God willing, I will continue to become a better person—not in spite of miscarriage or abortion, but because of them.

Despite our great loss, I can't imagine not experiencing the joy we felt over our child's conception. I can't imagine not sharing in the love of our child with our family and friends and of sharing that love with the world. I can't imagine not learning the difficult but beautiful lessons about life and death that we have had through this experience. Losing our child through miscarriage does not undo all that was done. Gabriel was conceived, he was loved, and I was blessed to carry him. We are all blessed to carry him now in our hearts until we meet him again. I want every woman to know that her child's life, her experience in carrying her daughter or son, is a gift—no matter how it's packaged.

I can see now that I am not the same woman I was before I experienced this miscarriage. Yes, my heart may be a little heavier with pain. Yes, my eyes have been opened to grief and loss, but I don't think those are bad things. I can think back to the Melissa I was before I married Ryan and the wife I was before I was blessed to be a mother, and in these instances and many others throughout my life, I was good. But I got better. By the grace of God, through every experience and every situation, I learned, I grew, and I changed. That is the transformational power of grief.

Yes, sadly, once we experience pain and trauma, we will never be the same, but God willing, we will walk through the dark tunnel of difficulty and loss to ultimately come out on the other side of life—a life that will never be the same but one that will have been transformed for the better. Till we meet again, our angel Gabriel, thank you for blessing us far greater than we ever could have imagined.

Thank you Dave for sharing your mother's sacred experience and her inspiring message, giving each of us all a small, but wonderful glimpse of what awaits in the next life.

Your book encourages us to ponder such questions as the following: When does life begin? Did we exist before our birth? Do we indeed live on after we pass from our mortal existence? What happens to the spirits of unborn children lost for whatever reason? In the afterlife, will we continue with the friendships and family relationships developed during our mortal lives? What are the implications of this book for the pro-life and pro-choice movements?

It is my sincere hope that all readers of *Extraordinary Comfort* will feel reassured with the knowledge that these little ones are not lost, but are safe in the loving care of the Savior, and I pray that each of you may experience positive transformational changes in your thinking about life's meanings associated with the loss of precious, unborn children.

Melissa Ohden
Founder of The Abortion Survivors Network
www.theabortionsurvivors.com

FURTHER INFORMATION

We created these next several pages to offer readers additional information about the number of miscarriages, abortions, and stillborn children in the United States and worldwide.

These stats are generally from government funded and supported resources.

MISCARRIAGE STATISTICS

Although statistics can vary slightly from one source to the next, here is a general account (based primarily on info provided by the March of Dimes) of the frequency of miscarriages in the United States:

- There are about 4.4 million confirmed pregnancies in the U.S. every year.

- 900,000 to 1 million of those end in pregnancy losses EVERY year.

- More than 500,000 pregnancies each year end in miscarriage (occurring during the first 20 weeks).

- Approximately 26,000 end in stillbirth (considered stillbirth after 20 weeks)

- Approximately 19,000 end in infant death during the first month.

- Approximately 39,000 end in infant death during the first year.

- Approximately 1 in 4 pregnancies end in miscarriage; some estimates are as high as 1 in 3. If you include loss that occurs before a positive pregnancy test, some estimate that 40% of all conceptions result in loss.

- Approximately 75% of all miscarriages occur in the first trimester.

- An estimated 80% of all miscarriages are single miscarriages. The vast majority of women suffering one miscarriage can expect to have a normal pregnancy next time.

- An estimated 19% of the adult population has experienced the death of a child (this includes miscarriages through adult-aged children).

ABORTION STATISTICS

- Abortions in the United States since 1973 (Roe Vs. Wade) through 2013: **56,405,766**

- Estimated number of abortions worldwide since 1980: **1.2 Billion**

- Estimated number of abortions worldwide annually: **40 Million**

- By age 45, one third of American women will have had at least one abortion.

- The U.S. has the highest abortion rate (19.4 per 1,000) of any western industrialized nation.

- 88.7% of all abortions take place by the twelfth week of pregnancy.

- Of the 18 regions divided by the United Nations, the regions with the highest number of abortions annually per 1000 women in the general population are:

    1. <u>Eastern Europe</u>: Belarus, Bulgaria, Czech Republic, Hungary, Poland, Romania, Russian Fereration, Slovakia, Ukraine. **43/1000 women**

    2. <u>Caribbean</u>: Aruba, Bahamas, Barbados, Cayman Islands, Cuba, Haiti, Jamaica, Puerto Rico. **36-43/1000 women**

3. <u>Eastern Africa</u>: Burundi, Ethiopia, Kenya, Madagascar, Mozambique. **36-43/1000 women**

4. <u>Southeastern Asia</u>: Cambodia, Indonesia, Laos, Malaysia, Myanmar, Phillipines, Singapore, Thailand, Vietnam. **36/1000 women**

Why Women Get Abortions

- Women who have never been married account for one-third of abortions in America.

- Less than 1% of all abortions take place because of rape and/or incest.

- Women give an average of 3.7 reasons why they are seeking an abortion, including the following:

  21%   Inadequate finances

  21%   Not ready for responsibility

  16%   Woman's life would be changed too much

  12%   Problems with relationships, unmarried

  11%   Too young and/or immature

  8%   Children are grown; she has all she wants

  3%   Baby has possible health problems

  <1%   Pregnancy caused by rape/incest

  4%   Other

RECOMMENDED RESOURCES

There are no stats that can measure grief felt annually or that count the number of dreams shattered because of the tragedies associated with abortion, miscarriage, and stillbirth. It's with the motive of offering comfort and help, especially to women and mothers, that this book was written. We invite all readers to make use of the resources provided here.

www.babiesremembered.org - We offer: Help in finding support, understanding, compassionate care, guidance, resources, networking links, speakers, perinatal loss consultants, excellent standards of bereavement care, literature, and so much more.

www.honoredbabies.org - Honored babies is primarily an organization for women as well as a support and resource organization for women whose babies have died. It also supports family members and informs the community, although that's not the focus.

www.mend.org - Mommies Enduring Neonatal Death (MEND) is a Christian, non-profit organization that reaches out to families who have suffered the loss of a baby through miscarriage, stillbirth, or early infant death.

www.nationalshare.org - Share Pregnancy and Infant Loss Support, Inc. Share has been helping bereaved families cope with infant loss since 1977.

www.theabortionsurvivors.com - Melissa Ohden is an abortion attempt survivor and is the Founder of The Abortion Survivors Network. She is a powerful advocate for the unborn.

www.missingGRACE.org - Missing GRACE Foundation is a national nonprofit organization that provides comfort, support, education and resources for families experiencing pregnancy loss, infant loss, infertility and adoption challenges.

www.hopexchange.com - HopeXchange offers a wealth of information for those who have been impacted by the grief of pregnancy loss. We provide educational and uplifting articles, booklets, pamphlets, and books, along with miscarriage FAQs and an extensive list of links and resources.

ABOUT THE AUTHOR

David C. Asay spent his professional life working in sales and sales management for several fortune 100 companies before becoming a successful business owner (now retired) living in suburban Atlanta. He is married to the former Pamela Vicchrilli. They have five children and 12 precious, beautiful, and nearly perfect grandchildren (including one not yet arrived!). With the knowledge that he also has a brother named Shawn, he now has four brothers and five sisters, making his family an even dozen, including his dad, Clifton W. Asay and mom, Mary Lou Gurr Asay.

His passions in life are his family, pursuing amateur archaeology from Egypt to Central America and Mexico, snorkeling, golf, fishing, jig-saw puzzles, and most of all, playing and snuggling with the grandbabies.

His love of travel and archaeology have provided him with the opportunity to produce two Mayan archaeological documentaries in the countries of Mexico and Guatemala.

daveasay@gmail.com — www.extraordinarycomfort.com